A LIFE WORTH

Abilities, interests ar
of a young disabl

A LIFE WORTH LIVING

Abilities, interests and travels of a young disabled man

JONATHAN COLCHESTER

Foreword by Professor Richard Edwards

Muscular
Dystrophy
Campaign

GREENRIDGES
PRESS

possum
Controls Limited

ISBN: 1 902019 06 7   ISBN13: 978-1-902019-06-2
First published January 2003
Reprinted January 2004
Reprinted January 2008

Published by:
Greenridges Press
an imprint of
Anne Loader Publications
13 Vale Road, Hartford,
Northwich, Cheshire CW8 1PL
Gt Britain
Tel: 01606 75660   Fax: 01606 77609
e-mail: anne@leoniepress.com
Website: www.anneloaderpublications.co.uk
www.leoniepress.com

Printed by:
Poplar Services, St Helens, Merseyside
Cover Lamination: The Finishing Touch, St Helens

Cover picture: the author aged 34, with Eagle Owl

Dedicated to Mum, Dad, sister
Christine and fellow MD sufferers

Foreword

It is a well established truism that doctors learn from their patients. The essential partnership based on mutual trust between clinical scientist and the patient studied has served medicine and the public very well in providing cures or effective treatments for many diseases. While persons disabled by one or other of the muscular dystrophies have yet to be cured, they can and must receive the best possible treatment and care for components of their problems as and when they appear. This book is a revealing account of a young person who by any standards is a very remarkable individual and who has, with a light hand, charted the course of progress of his disabilities and how he and his family have coped in the hope that others may find practical assistance.

Jonathan Colchester is clear thinking, determined, blessed with artistic talents, and possessed of deeply spiritual love and empathy with his fellow human beings and wildlife. He is blessed too with a loving supportive family and circle of friends.

You will be almost breathless reading his book which is proof (if ever there was need of it) that the full life is lived by and through an active mind. Undeterred by his physical disability, Jonathan planned an amazing range of journeys in Europe and North America which he describes in fluent prose and beautifully executed paintings and drawings.

What have I learned from knowing Jonathan over more than 20 years? I think I have been impressed more than anything with his obvious enjoyment of life and ability to accept that "the best thing about the future is that it only comes one day at a time" – a message that is worth learning by every one of us in this age of big uncertainties. It is a privilege to be asked to write a Foreword for a book but it is an exceptional honour to be associated in this way with the author of a book which will certainly be an inspiration to all.

Generously, Jonathan has determined that profits from the sale of this book should go to support research into improving care and hope of cure of the muscular dystrophies – an aim which is clearly important to both of us.

R. H. T. Edwards

Emeritus Professor of Research and Development in Health and Social Care, University of Wales, formerly Professor of Medicine, University of Liverpool and before that, Professor of Human Metabolism, University College London.

Introduction

Since meeting Jonathan Colchester in 1987 we have witnessed a physical decline due to his muscular dystrophy that is both alarming and heartbreaking. Yet, as this book so powerfully demonstrates, Jonathan's strength of character and unbreakable spirit shine through every twist and turn of his life. These qualities continue to sustain him against apparently overwhelming odds.

Jonathan is a very special young man. His experiences might have been so limited by his disability but despite his illness, he has succeeded in packing more into his life than many a more able bodied contemporary. In addition, he has achieved an understanding and acceptance of his own situation that is far beyond the expectations of many an observer.

The remarkable accomplishments described in this autobiographical account are due to the support of his dedicated parents and family; the skill of Jonathan's doctors and carers; the encouragement of friends; and Jonathan's strong and personal Christian faith. It is his daily close relationship with Jesus that, above all else, has enabled Jonathan *to run the race* (Bible, Hebrews 12.1) so far and so well.

Our expectation is as Jonathan's; that he will with his Lord's help, finish the race and win the prize.

John and Marion Hayes
Barrow 1987 - 1994

"The fruit of the Spirit is love, joy, patience..." You are not long in Jonathan's presence before you are struck by the joy and patience that come from within him. He is the first to acknowledge that this is God's doing. Patience is not a hope-

iii

less resignation to a cruel fate, but a positive rising to the challenges that come our way. It is the opposite of despondence and is imbued with hope.

It was my privilege for many years to minister to the Colchester family, and Jonathan in particular. We shared enthusiasms for art, music, ornithology and wild places. We shared a love of God's Word and many times we knew God to be close to us. Jonathan has been a great inspiration and blessing to me. His book is called "A life worth living". What he shows to many of us is "a faith worth having."

Canon J. A. Malbon

Author's Preface

My primary purpose of writing this autobiography is to help and encourage Muscular Dystrophy sufferers, carers, doctors, therapists and the like; all those who need to be aware of and come into contact with this genetic disability.

I also want to try to demonstrate that it is possible to overcome severe disability and lead a fulfilling life while at the same time adapting to the changing patterns the disability imposes.

J A Colchester
November 2002

Acknowledgements

I would like to say how grateful I am to the following people:

Mum, Dad and sister Christine for their love, encouragement and practical support.

Mum for typing part of the original manuscript.

Paul for his invaluable help in scanning in Mum's typing into the computer and patience in typing my dictations.

The Physios at Hebden Green, Winsford, Pat Bennett, Kate Fox, for their attention to my wellbeing.

To Professor Edwards and his MD research team I will be eternally grateful.

And for the many people who came in and out of my life and in doing so helped me on life's journey.

Finally - three maxims which have always inspired me:

Inch by inch it's a sinch

If you believe it you can achieve it

If it's going to be it's up to me

Contents

Chapter 1

The Formative Years

I was born by forceps delivery on 10th May 1967 at Clatterbridge Hospital, Wirral at 1.45pm, and weighed 7lb 2oz. My parents told me I was a good baby, slept well and was always happy and contented. We came home from hospital to Whitby, Ellesmere Port, where we were living at the time. I started walking at about 15 months old.

In 1969 we moved from Whitby to Queens Park Chester, where my sister Christine was born at home on Saturday, 10th January 1969. Christine was a normal delivery and was born at 2.30a.m. Mum remembers clearly me going off to bed on the Friday evening and when I woke up I was taken to see my new sister. Christine did not need much sleep; she was walking at nine months old and was always on the go.

It was very handy living in Queens Park very close to town and so convenient for Mum when she was pushing Christine and me to school. When I was three I started school at Abbey Gate. For the first six months I went during the mornings only, then after six

Me, aged one.

1

months I attended full-time.

About this time, my parents bought a touring caravan and we had many holidays touring England and Wales, going to some very interesting places. The holidays were really good fun, full of adventure, particularly the beaches with their ample opportunities for building sand castles, splashing about in the sea and of course, burying Dad in the sand.

When I was two years old I used to fall a lot; people would say "put your hands out to save yourself" but I found it difficult to do so. I hurt myself many times, particularly my forehead – it was always in the same position. I was also told that when I fell over and attempted to stand up I used to do this from a cautious crawling position, that is by crawling my hands from my ankles upwards I was able to lever myself to a standing position.

In 1972 when I was five my parents took me to see a GP who

Me, aged four, and Christine

was obviously extremely astute and advised them to see a consultant in Chester. He was, so I am told, rather blunt with my parents and was quite clear that Duchenne Muscular Dystrophy was present. He advised us that we should attend a hospital in Liverpool for a muscle biopsy which was taken from the top of my left leg near my thigh. In those days this procedure required a general anaesthetic – it was an operation – and I remember clearly being gassed and the

2

taste of the rubber mask over my face. The diagnosis resulting from the biopsy confirmed that I had Duchenne Muscular Dystrophy. This revelation was to prove very distressing for all my family. It took a long time to come to terms with this news, which is understandable.

To quote my Mum's words years later: "Seeing a robust and healthy youngster and hearing the prognosis was hard to reconcile." However, Mum could talk freely about how she felt. Her mood was one of

Me, aged five, and Christine

resignation and a determination to take things one day at a time. Dad, on the other hand, found the diagnosis more difficult to accept and even harder to talk about.

Our summer holiday that year was to the Greek Island of Corfu, staying near Benitses, in an apartment with friends called the Andersons. The apartment had a balcony which overlooked the Ionian Sea. There are many memories which are easily brought to mind when I recall the holiday. On one occasion we visited a monastery on Mouse Island, a short boat trip from Corfu. The buildings were white-washed and stood out, a typical feature of Greek architecture. There were also a few trees and lovely flowers on the island. It was an island that exuded peace, an ideal place for quiet reflection. On another day I remember sightseeing around Corfu Town, the island's capital and having a drink in one of the cafés overlooking the cricket pitch, no doubt one of the more genteel exports from Britain! Towering above this ground was the castle looking majestically over the town. Another day trip took us to the coastal village of Benitsis, a small place then, but bigger now, swelled by tourism. It was here I bought the purchase of a lifetime, an inflatable fish with a hole in it which fitted over your head whilst swimming. This forerunner of 'Jaws', menacingly coloured in reddy pink with yellow scales and a beady eye, served me well on many holidays. My final mem-

Pictured with my parents and my sister at a wedding

ory of Corfu was at a Greek taverna near our apartment when my Mum was chosen by the restaurant staff to dance the night away to the strains of "Zorba the Greek". On the way back at the end of the evening we saw fireflies lighting the way.

In December of 1972 we moved from Queens Park, Chester to Great Barrow, some eight miles due east of Chester. One memory I can recall from this time was having a particularly nasty fall at school and being taken to the headmistress, Mrs Parry. I don't remember precisely what she did other than wipe away my tears with a perfumed handkerchief and be extremely kind and understanding. Mrs Parry was also our elocution teacher, she taught us how to speak "proper" and entertained us with stories she made up about a monkey called Mancho, and all his adventures and escapades. She was a great raconteur. It was while I was at Abbey Gate that my special friendship with Edward Maddox began. Edward became my minder, shielding me from the threat of being knocked over as pupils rushed by on the stairs and in the corridors. Edward was a great help then and remains a good friend now. I had a happy time at Abbey Gate: everyone was very friendly there and I remember how kind Mrs Parry was, she was a real friend.

Other adventures I enjoyed occurred whilst staying at our static caravan in Anglesey. We had exchanged a touring van for the static in 1972. Let me set the scene. The caravan was located on Anglesey's Holy Island a few miles due west of Holyhead, perched on a hill overlooking the sea and cliffs. You could also see the Snowdon mountain range clearly in good weather. Our stretch of beach was called 'Porthdafach', a lovely bay. In one corner of the bay sat a small, dark grey stone structure which was used when smuggling was commonplace. Near our caravan stood a two-metre mound of rock which I liked to scale. For a five-year-old this was a challenge; coupled with my weakness, the elation I felt on reaching the top was equivalent to reaching the summit of Snowdon! Flanking the caravan site were carpets of gorse which my sister and I would roam through. In one particular section there was a bowl-like depression with a slab of rock set into it – a perfect spot to build a den. Occasionally, I would wander off on my own expeditions of discovery in and around the caravan site. I can recall a few times getting into difficulty when, having lost my balance, I struggled to get up again, but I always managed to redeem the situation and myself. If we weren't in the gorse we were in the sea, especially on warm sunny days, although the sea was perishing cold – particularly on the initial immersion – but you soon became acclimatised! Even though on getting out your body was blue, your limbs were numb and your eyes were sore, it was pleasant nonetheless. Another activity which I enjoyed was messing about in my dinghy with the family.

Also when I was five I had a bicycle with stabilizers and managed to ride around to see my friends – Paul, Martin, Jamie and Edward. We had many adventures around my home village of Barrow. Near my house there was a field with potatoes growing in it and we used to walk over the field frequently. I can recall falling over a lot because the furrows made me off balance. My friends, rather impatiently, would walk on ahead of me but wait until I eventually caught up with them. But changes were afoot!

Chapter 2

Signs of Change

When not in the sea at Anglesey, swimming at the local baths was a physical activity I always enjoyed on a regular basis: the buoyancy and freedom which the water provided was great. Mum used to take me swimming to Chester College Baths and I managed to attain a ten-metre badge. Physically too, I was able to walk up and down stairs and dress myself and about this time I had joined the Cub Scouts in Tarvin. I managed to join in with some of the activities and observed other activities such as erecting tents. I also watched other Cubs clearing out a very dirty stream.

As time went by I found it more and more difficult to walk up and down stairs which posed particular difficulties at school. The general geography of the Abbey Gate School coupled with an increasing fear of being knocked over made a move necessary. So I continued at Abbey Gate until my ninth birthday before moving on to a special school for the physically disabled in Winsford called Hebden Green. I had my first session of physiotherapy at Hebden Green which involved stretching and twisting, and bending my legs, arms and feet into various positions and angles. I also stood up on a standing frame and was able to do schoolwork whilst standing.

Towards the end of 1976 I began to use a wheelchair occasionally at the Hebden Green School and had a major buggy at home permanently. I used the buggy only when we went for weekends away or on day trips out, when I got fatigued and had general muscle aches.

My friends at school were Tony Whelan, Paul Berry and Duncan Firmin who all had Duchenne Muscular Dystrophy. I had two other friends, one called Jonathan Gleave who had Muscular Atrophy and John Stott.

On 3rd October 1976 I went away with the school for a week's holiday to Llandudno. This was the first time that I had been away from home on my own and I considered it a new adventure. We stayed at a special school in Llandudno, and went on a number of trips out. One particular trip was up the Great Orme which is a large coastal limestone cliff. To get to the top of the cliff you had to go in a tram. It was very cold, wet and windy so we all enjoyed a nice hot cup of tea at the top – the best drink of the day! We also visited Llandudno light-house on the Orme which was a fascinating and interesting experience. We went outside the lighthouse and observed the steep cliff and fabulous sea birds.

On another day we drove to Snowdonia where the scenery and the autumn colours and textures were beautiful. On this journey we visited Llechwedd slate caverns and went on a train through the cavern which was fascinating, seeing the slate and rock formation. There were models of men carrying out various jobs in the cavern, such as hammering away at the slate. We also watched a man cutting a piece of slate and the technique he used. It is the largest working slate mine in Wales. On the journey back from this particular trip we stopped off at the Swallow Falls, it was a beautiful waterfall.

In the following year, 1977, on 5th February, a few friends and I went to Jonathan Gleave's birthday party. A good time was had by all. A few days later tragedy struck. Jonathan was involved in an horrific accident at his home when the lift which had been installed for him malfunctioned, causing him fatal injuries. At his party just days earlier a few of us had used the lift.

I can recall after Jonathan's death on a few occasions lying in bed reflecting on life, about living and dying. Living and then dying like that, without an explanation, doesn't really make sense. There had to be something more. This seemed like a barrier at the time. Later this barrier came down.

At the age of nine and a half I sensed that I would be in a wheelchair permanently in the near future, because my legs were getting weaker – and by the age of ten this was the case. I accepted being in a wheelchair straight away and was never apprehensive about it. I remember vividly the last time that I walked. I was coming out of the Cub Hut in the evening and slipped as I came down the last step. My legs went from under me and I fell in the same manner about four times before I reached home. A friend of mine called Jamie was staying with us that night, he was interested in making electronic gadgetry.

After falling over so many times my legs felt quite painful. Next day I went to the hospital for an X-ray to find out if I had broken anything but everything was all right. My legs were now too weak to stand up. At this time I was able to propel myself in a wheelchair even though it was slow going.

In 1978 I went on another school holiday to a Youth Hostel called Legge House down in Wiltshire. I borrowed one of the school's electric chairs for the trip. We visited the city of Salisbury on one outing and went into the cathedral. It was well equipped with a ramp to get in. Salisbury Cathedral is impressive: it has the tallest spire in the country. Just outside the town of Roman Salisbury we visited Old Sarum which is the remains of an old castle. I drove the wheelchair around part of it, and it was very bumpy going over the drawbridge. My friends complained about my wheelchair driving – I was pretty dangerous at that time!

On another day out we visited Bristol and went to the Zoo, which had good facilities for wheelchairs. We saw the majestic White Tiger – a wonderful creature. We drove our chairs over the Clifton Suspension Bridge a number of times. The bridge is an amazing feat of engineering, designed and built by that great Victorian engineer Isambard Kingdom Brunel.

Later we went to the Stonehenge ancient monument which is a very unusual arrangement of stone monoliths. On one hillside we saw a white horse embedded into the hillside with chalk rock. Another day we visited Swindon and looked around the Great Western Railway Museum which is fascinating, seeing all the steam trains and elegant carriages. Whilst in this area we went into a fairly large shopping centre that had ramp escalators; my friends and I had great fun going up and down them. We visited an RAF base where we saw many helicopters such as the Wessex, the standard search and rescue chopper. The Sea Cadets took us on a guided tour of the base. I had a really great week's holiday.

At this time I was only able to dress and undress myself slightly and needed a bit of help.

In 1978 my father was made works manager at ICI's Fleetwood factory and we had to leave Chester. We moved to The Coach House in Little Eccleston on the Fylde. I went to a special school a few miles away called Singleton Hall which was set in nice lush green grounds; we often saw pheasants strutting about. One year, I took part in the Christmas Panto, *Cinderella*, when I played the part of an ugly sister. Another year I was the King in *Sleeping Beauty*. I really enjoyed acting in these plays.

I was still able to propel myself around the school slowly. My chair had removable arm rests so I could transfer myself from the chair on to my bed: I gradually lowered the top half of my body onto the bed then Mum lifted my legs on. This was quite useful for a time but then later it became a more and more difficult manoeuvre.

Grandma and Grandad came to stay with us for a few days; one day during their visit Grandad and I did some painting and drawing together. He inspired me and a learnt a lot from him.

In 1980 while I was still at Singleton Hall I had a physiotherapist who came to the house once a week, as I didn't have enough physiotherapy at school. This physiotherapist was also involved with the local horse riding for the disabled. One day she invited my sister and me to a show jumping event at Charnock Richard in Lancashire. We travelled on a coach with other disabled people from the Blackpool area. I had to be held at times when the coach went round sharp corners. It was a great day out which I thoroughly enjoyed; there were a lot of stalls and displays around the show jumping arena. I was introduced to David Broome, the famous show jumper.

I designed a ramp for the local disabled people to get on to the horse for their riding sessions.

I was able to propel a normal wheelchair until September 1980 then it became very difficult for me; I couldn't propel it very fast anyway but managed to get where I was going in the end. Whilst I was in Blackpool I joined the PHAB club at Lytham St Anne's. The initials stand for 'Physically Handicapped and Able-Bodied' and it is an organisation which meets weekly. Most of the people were older than me. We played games, chatted and listened to music.

After two years at Singleton Hall I transferred to another special school called Highfurlong in the September of 1980. I stopped having the physiotherapist coming to the house as that was taken care of at school. When I started at this school my knees were quite bent and had to be stretched daily – this was very painful. Often I had ice wrapped in a towel, which helped to relieve the pain. After a couple of months of stretching, my knee became a lot straighter and it wasn't painful any more. I took part in the annual Christmas Panto which was great fun.

Next door to where I lived there was a field and the annual Great Eccleston show was held there, run by the Horticultural

11

Society. This was a great event held twice a year. It featured a tractor pull competition, when the competing tractors pulled huge weights on a trailer.

One Sunday at St. Anne's Church, Great Eccleston, I met a lady called Mrs Clegg who was physically handicapped – having had both legs amputated, she had spent six months in hospital. Shortly before this her husband had died. My sister Christine and I became very friendly with her and we used to do jobs to help her with shopping and similar things. She is a wonderful courageous person, very independent and manages to live on her own – absolutely amazing! Some time after her operation she felt God calling her to do something for the young people in the area and she decided to start a club at her house, which was a great success. We used to meet on Tuesday evenings and we had a good time. We played games, cooked, painted, and so on. I visited Mrs Clegg after school in my electric chair most days. I was able to open her gate by parking the chair side-on by the gate and reaching to open the latch. I then pushed my chair into the gate and opened it. The BBC did a TV programme called *Unlucky for Some*, in which the club participated. My sister and I were on the programme which was fun and a new experience.

In the winter of 1980 I attended confirmation classes and was confirmed on my 14th birthday. All the family came for the day and we had a very pleasant time together. The Bishop of Lancaster took the confirmation service which was a memorable occasion. After being confirmed, I joined the Youth Fellowship group. On a Sunday evening we used to play games, talk together and watch films. In the summer we visited the Priory Sacred Monastery near Lancaster on a blazing hot day. We went on a long walk in the lovely countryside. In the late afternoon we gathered together and a chap played the guitar. We sang various gospel songs including "Seek Ye First the Kingdom of God". Everyone had a good time. We had a barbecue and later we walked round part of the monastery which was a very peaceful place with beautiful wooden panelling. There were about a hundred people present from the various churches in the area.

In the winter of 1980 I joined the lst Great Eccleston Scouts which I enjoyed very much. The Scout leader used to call and collect me and take me to the Scout meetings. I took part in some of the activities such as cooking, which was enjoyable. I was the Secretary for the Scouts in order to organise a Raft Race on the River Wyre at Little Eccleston, just down the road from us. I don't remember who won, but our boat sank! After a time I stopped going to Scouts as it was much too cold for me in the Scout Hut.

When I was at Highfurlong School I took part in Sports Days. These were organised through BSAD (the British Sports Association for Disabled) and were held at different venues throughout the North West. People came from miles around to participate and everyone had a great time. Events I took part in ranged from Connect 4, to draughts and table skittles. The competitions were organised in leagues, the winners progressing through preliminary rounds to a final. Another sports activity which was really enjoyable at school was a form of ice hockey played with plastic sticks, and a circular puck made out of plastic. It was played either on the playground or on a shiny indoor floor. The dining area was fine. It was no place for the faint-hearted, with wheelchairs clattering and crashing around! Without the use of an electric chair in school I would have been unable to participate in the hockey. I never made it to the Olympic trials... Oh well!!

In April 1981 Prince Charles came to re-open the Grand Theatre in Blackpool. I and some other people were invited by the council to see him. We were fortunate to be in the front when Prince Charles was on a walkabout and he stopped to talk to my Mum and me, which was very exciting. I was on one of the pictures in the local paper.

Early in 1981 our doctor wrote a letter to University College Hospital, London and we heard they were doing some research into Muscular Dystrophy. This was just at the time when the hospital wanted people to participate in some research. Our first visit coincided with the wedding of Prince Charles and Lady Diana. I was invited to be in the forecourt of Buckingham Palace. This invitation came about because tickets were given to the Muscular Dystrophy Association of Great Britain who distributed them to people who applied for them. When the Royal Family returned from the service at St Paul's Cathedral we had a wonderful view of all the carriages, which were only a few feet away from us. This was a very special day and the atmosphere was great. When the wedding party came on to the balcony of the Palace we had an excellent position on the front row. In the evening we got a taxi to University College Hospital. It was very difficult for Mum to get me in the taxi, as I was very heavy at that time. It was a juggling act for her to try and balance the wheelchair at the same time as holding me, but of course we managed.

On our first visit to the hospital we spent ten days there. I had blood and urine tests, and went on a machine which scanned the fat layers around my body. I also had a body scan, breathing tests, a muscle biopsy and went on a machine which measured the strength of my hands and legs. My hands and legs were wired up to electrodes; this apparatus made my hands move involuntarily, which tingled – a very strange sensation!

I was on a meat-free diet for four days. When tests were not being carried out Mum and I went on trips out. We visited London Zoo and saw Chi-Chi, the beautiful Giant Panda. We had several trips to Covent Garden, a lovely old market place, with lots of super modern shops in keeping with the character of the place.

The London Transport Museum, which is in Covent Garden, was a very interesting place to visit, seeing how the different methods of transport have changed over the years and have progressed from the stage coach to the motor car.

I subsequently went down to London every six weeks for a series of tests over a period of two years. During this time I was on lots of different trial tablets. I travelled to London on the train which was an experience and a half! We asked for assistance to help get me on and off the train and on a number of occasions no British Rail official met us off the train. Fortunately, there was always someone kind enough to give us assistance.

On my second trip to London I went to Northwick Park Hospital, Harrow and was taken there by taxi. I had a test to measure the potassium levels in my body, and had to go into a huge chamber. I lay on a bed inside this chamber for about 45 minutes. The doors on the chamber were about 10 inches thick and bolted from behind, in all there was 10 tons of equipment surrounding me with a small port-hole for observation at one end. The people in the hospital dealing with me were extremely kind and friendly. Whilst I was in the chamber I had a Carpenters tape playing which helped to pass the time away. After being in this chamber, the following morning I had a radio-active cocktail and a blood test.

At this time I was put on a very strict diet of six hundred calories a day; my weight was eight and a half stone. As an incentive to lose weight Mum paid me £1 for every pound I lost, but if I put weight on I would then owe Mum.

At this time the local Muscular Dystrophy group gave me a Flowtron machine, which helps to stimulate circulation. The parts fitted on my arms and legs and were electrically controlled. This was useful to me but I was expected to be on the machine for a couple of hours a day, which was not always possible.

In August 1982 we left the Fylde, and moved back to Chester to our new home called Oak Bank.

When moving into a new house there are always jobs to do. Dad had asked around for a joiner to help out and was given the name and telephone number of a man called Ron Baxter. Ron, in addition to helping out with various jobs, became a good friend. As well as repairing things around the house he would also design and make things for me. This started with a tipping trailer that was attached to the rear of the wheelchair. The tipping mechanism was activated by me pulling a piece of string using one hand. He also made me a larger tray for working on, mainly painting, and reading boards to make life easier, which were an enormous help. Later on he would often accompany me to our local pub for a pint or two; the journey back in the electric chair was a bit erratic to say the least! I was glad that there were no policemen about with breathalysers in those days.

Ron invited me to celebrate both his daughters' weddings. Both had their receptions at the local pub, which by now had become a hotel, and I was invited along for a drink. The evening was a disco held in a nearby community centre and Ron kindly invited me there too. An entry in my diary records the dance of the "wheel-a-boogie-woogie for the electric chair" and "...danced the night away". I nearly burned the motors out!

Chapter 3

Barbados Holiday, July 1976

We were all excited about going to Barbados in July 1976. I was nine years old and still on my feet. We had a really super holiday – almost like one would imagine paradise to be.

We hired a Mini Moke in which to tour around the island, which was perfect. On one occasion we visited Welshman Hall Gully, where the vegetation was hanging down like stalactites – the further the family and I walked into the gully the darker it became. It was rather an eerie experience and quite a long walk for me – I was fairly tired after it. The Queen had visited this gully the year before. We also visited the beautiful Andromeda Gardens. There was a pond which was full of frogs, and it was fun trying to count them all! There were many exotic trees, shrubs and plants including the Bird of Paradise plants to see.

Driving around the island in a Mini Moke was quite a fun experience. We visited Sam Lord's Castle, a pirate's castle, which had beautiful gardens with lovely water features; from here we could see the Atlantic rollers crashing on to the beach. There are lots of sugar plantations in Barbados. We also saw, on another part of the island, a long avenue of magnificent mahogany trees – an increasingly expensive timber for quality furniture.

Northern Barbados is fairly hilly and the area is known as "The Highlands". Bridgetown is the capital of the island.

Whilst driving around one day I observed a mongoose, an

17

animal which was introduced to the island a number of years ago to kill snakes. On the Atlantic side there are some unusual rock formations which have been caused by the sea erosion. There is a lot of poverty in Barbados; some people lived in corrugated shacks but they seemed very happy, even though they had few possessions.

On another day we took a trip to another island in the West Indies called St Lucia. It's a volcanic island with huge banana plantations. We flew from Bridgetown to St Lucia's capital, Castries, and climbing above the town in a mini-bus, we saw some military arsenals that were in use during the bloody wars when the British fought against the French.

There was the same poverty in St Lucia that we had seen in Barbados. On one part of the island women were washing their clothes in a stream. Later we stopped off at a little fishing village where young people were asking the tourists to throw coins into the sea so that they could dive in for them.

Above the fishing village are two peaks called the Petones near to Souffriere volcano. We walked to the volcano which was exciting and frightening at the same time. It was very difficult for me to walk around the bubbling pools of lava, if you slipped you would end up in the pool of boiling lava, not a nice experience! The air was heavy with the smell of sulphur. I had a swim in St Lucia, where the sand was volcanic and black. The sand hurt our bare feet – it was absolutely baking because of the intense heat of the sun. It was a relief to get into the water to cool down! On the journey back to Castries airport we stopped off at a small bay where the film *Dr. Dolittle* was filmed.

Our apartment in Barbados overlooked the Caribbean Sea and there was a balcony on which we had our breakfast most mornings. We self-catered while we were there and it was fun shopping in the colourful markets, both indoor and outdoor, with their exotic and varied range of fruit and vegetables. We had a lot of fruit such as mangos, water melons, paw paw and breadfruit. My sister Christine and I enjoyed the fruit punch cocktails, obtained from the Koos Koos thatch-roofed cocktail bar and restaurant. Near to the bar area we often heard the sound of a steel band adding to the atmosphere of the place. A Banana Bird came on the balcony on a number of occasions, it was beautiful with very colourful plumage.

We visited Bridgetown twice. On one of these visits we saw the famous cricket ground where the team representing the West Indies play – our equivalent of Lords – and where many a famous test match has been played out.

It was a truly wonderful holiday – quite unique!

Chapter 4

First Trip to America, April 1979

West Coast, California, Arizona, Nevada

When we went abroad in April 1979 I was 12 years old and in a wheelchair permanently. We flew from Gatwick airport and after a few formalities Mum and I went on a golf-buggy type vehicle through the airport and got out quite near to the plane. There was a passageway right to the plane called a Jetway. These Jetways are very useful and are a great help. The wheelchair went into the hold of the plane with the luggage. It was important to make sure that the wheelchair went into the plane and that it came out at the next airport.

The aeroplane touched down at Salt Lake City, Utah. We had to get out for a while but this time there was no Jetway so I had to be lifted down the steps of the plane. I think more airports should have Jetways for people who have difficulties with disabilities – it makes it very much easier. It is an area where money should be spent to provide more facilities for the disabled.

On the first day of our holiday we visited the Hollywood Bowl in the Hollywood Hills, a huge auditorium used for concerts and the like. Nearby was the famous large Hollywood sign which appears like a great billboard embedded in the hillside. Next port of call was the well-known farmers' market selling an abundance of fruit and vegetables. I picked up an enormous banana, the biggest I have ever seen! Another 'first',

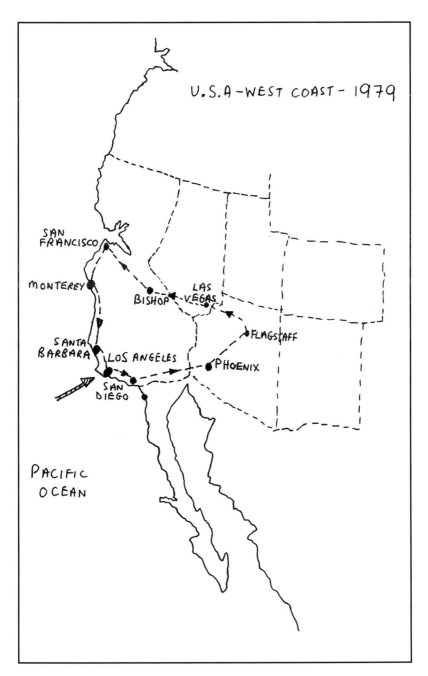

incredibly, was a pet shop selling peaked caps to be worn by dogs.

Later we visited the enormous Universal Studios where such films as *Jaws 1* and *Jaws 2* were filmed. We saw how the *Bionic Woman* and the *Six Million Dollar Man* series were filmed and how all the special effects are achieved. We also saw how many other films are made and how they build various props and mock buildings to achieve stunts – it was very interesting. I travelled around the studio park in a trolley car, one of four which were coupled together like train carriages. It took a couple of steps to get into the trolley but there was no difficulty, I could balance all right on the seat of the vehicle and didn't need to be held in place at all. At one part of the park the train travelled towards a rickety-looking timber bridge and as it approached the middle section the whole bridge structure began to collapse below us, thankfully the effect, although realistic, only allowed the train to drop for a few feet, but not before several gasps of fear had been heard. In another area of the park there was a large pool resembling a harbour with a jetty. In the centre of the pool was anchored a small boat with two dummies inside, but this was not obvious at first glance – they looked like men. Then, suddenly the profile of a shark's fin appeared tracking towards the boat, eventually flipping the boat over and causing it to sink. For a moment the shark disappeared out of sight and then it leapt out of the water very close to where our train was parked, its mouth gushing with water that thoroughly soaked some, including me! We were all scared out of our wits! It was while we were walking around that a familiar face greeted me and shook me by the hand – it was none other than Mary Shelley's Frankenstein's Monster.

We visited Disneyland, the famous theme park. We went on a number of enjoyable rides such as the "Journey into Space", the monorail (for an aerial view of the Park), and a submarine ride, which involved Dad lifting me down a narrow hatch into the sub. The ride simulated an underwater adventure with realistic sculptures of coral reefs, sharks, octopi and such like. My favourite ride was "The Pirates of the Caribbean", a gondola-shaped boat which sailed around a water course. Loud explosions happened intermittently as depth charges sent plumes of water into the air. The pirate figures looked realistic along with their ships and trinkets of golden sovereigns and treasure. "A-hah me hearties," as Long John Silver would say!

They had a few good facilities for disabled people: flat surfaces for negotiating my wheelchair, and the mono-rail had a ramp-escalator, a flat plane on the move which on this occasion, an official had switched off thinking it would be easier for us to reach the level of the railway. The facilities were generally good. I had to be lifted onto the rides.

There is so much to see and do, you could spend several days here. We had lunch at Denny's Restaurant, Anaheim, where there was a step to get into the place, but once inside there was sufficient room to get my wheelchair underneath the dining table, making it a lot easier for me to feed myself.

The following day we motored south of Anaheim to Mission Valley just outside San Diego. We travelled on a Grey line coach to Tijuana, Mexico on a shopping tour. As we approached Tijuana the coach driver said, "We are now approaching the land of the Margaritas, Senoritas and the Smelly Feeters." There was a lot of poverty in Tijuana. We walked around a number of unusual gift shops selling items made locally, such as onyx goods and sombreros. I had to be lifted into the coach but there were no problems and it was nice to see a different way of life and culture.

After driving back to our base in San Diego, the following day we travelled eastwards to the City of Phoenix in the State of Arizona. On the journey through much rugged and rocky terrain the outcrops looked quite barren from a distance, but closer inspection revealed an abundance of various types of cacti. In another area of this desert region I observed the landscape being transformed by irrigation which promoted patches of green in an otherwise parched and seemingly lifeless terrain. From Phoenix, we proceeded north to Flagstaff, a distance of some 100 miles and en route saw the enormous Saguaro Cactus. In Flagstaff we stayed at a Travel Lodge for an overnight stop, arriving mid-morning to book in, before travelling on to see the Grand Canyon National Park. On arriving there my Dad put me on the wall overlooking the Canyon which was quite a hair-raising experience: I had never been so scared before in my life!

The Grand Canyon is a mile deep, eight miles across and approximately 200 miles long. Its scenery and colours are out of this world – absolutely fantastic – the rocks are a mixture of reds, purples and browns. It was a most awe-inspiring sight, and words cannot express the beauty of this place. We stayed on for a while to watch the sunset producing a wonderful kaleidoscope of colours. The Navajo Indians inhabit this region on a reservation.

The next day we travelled from Flagstaff to Las Vegas in the State of Nevada, and stopped off at the massive Hoover Dam, which provides hydroelectric power for Las Vegas and the surrounding area – it is an interesting sight and a grand engineering feat. With all the cement used in the building of the dam you could build a path across North America. The dam, on the Colorado River, created a huge reservoir called Lake Mead.

We arrived in Las Vegas in the afternoon. It is known as the gambling and entertainment capital of the world, set in the middle of the desert. I have never seen so many gambling halls, casinos and huge hotels in a town before. We stayed on The Strip in Las Vegas which is the main street running through, where all the famous hotels and casinos stand. When you walk off the street and into Caesar's Palace Hotel you are transported on a moving flat escalator which gently curves and rises until it reaches the threshold of the hotel foyer. It is a few minutes travelling on the escalator which enables you to view the outside world through what seems like a glass tube and at the same time hear over the public address system the words, "I, Caesar welcome you." Another hotel we visited was the Metro Goldwyn Meyer – or M.G.M. It had an enclosed area resembling a shopping arcade, part of which provided a photo opportunity. You could have your photograph taken beside a live young male lion, which of course is the famous logo which introduces any M.G.M. film production. Dad, at this time, was about to take a snap when he was advised not to, they were after all, trying to make an honest buck! They were, however, kind enough to offer me a large photograph of their lion. In the M.G.M. Hotel I had a huge ice cream at Swenson's, a parlour famous for its ice cream. The one I had was packed full of chocolate, raspberries and other delicious fruits which were delightful to the palate, but far too much for me to scoff!! On one occasion we strolled into a casino which my sister and I were not allowed to enter because we were too young, but we didn't realise that until we were half way in – quite an experience! We stayed in Las Vegas for two nights before moving on to Death Valley.

Death Valley is the lowest point in America and very hot indeed, 120 degrees Fahrenheit, in a desert land with lots of surprising rock features and a few hotels. We stopped off at an hotel called Furnace Creek, which is a very apt name.

We drove from the lowest point in America to the highest in one day, which is amazing. At one point we came off the main highway onto a beaten track and travelled for about half a mile which was an eerie experience since we were in the middle of nowhere in this desertscape. It was very inhospitable, and not a place where you would want to break down, what with rattle snakes and who knows what else! Later, we passed a salt lake called Owens Lake; it was hot and the surrounding air was cold so the lake was steaming which was an amazing sight. From this point could be seen Mt. Whitney, at 14,494ft. the highest point in continental America, outside Alaska. The mountain looked spectacular to behold with its snow-capped peak.

We stayed at a place called Bishop for one night in a Travel Lodge, in a ground floor room. All the hotels in America offered good facilities with lifts, or we had rooms which were on the ground floor, which was very useful.

That evening for our meal, in a Swiss chalet style building, we enjoyed our first prime rib of beef, a succulent steak and an enormous portion at that. The knife slid through the meat like butter! There was just too much on the plate to eat and a doggy bag was no use as we were travelling all the next day.

We drove from Bishop into San Francisco, and on the way we travelled through nice sunny weather. We tried to get into Yosemite National Park but unfortunately it was closed to trucking because the spring snows had not yet melted, so we had to re-route this part of the journey to San Francisco via the ski resort of Lake Tahoe. As we approached it we drove through a severe snow storm. We heard on the radio that drivers would need chains around their tyres and this made us a little apprehensive, thinking that we would not be able to pass through Tahoe. But we did manage and we continued driving until the snow began to clear, which was a relief. Eventually we came into the city of San Francisco over the Bay Bridge and stayed at Fisherman's Wharfs Travel Lodge. It was interesting walking around the wharf, smelling all the freshly-caught fish, lobsters, crabs, clams and mussels. We had a good look at the many kinds of fishing vessels.

We journeyed into downtown San Francisco on one of the city's famous cable cars. I found it quite hard balancing on the cable car, particularly when my Dad was taking photographs. The cable cars tumbled "to the stars" as the Tony Bennett song goes, and ours certainly tumbled up and down the very steep inclines at a steady 9½ mph. As the driver put on the brakes I banged the back of my head which made me jump out of my skin. In the afternoon we set off to stroll up Lombard Street, which is known as the crookedest in the world and curves around lovely flower filled beds – but it was too steep, so after a while we decided to return later in the car and then drove down it.

Another day our travels took us over the Golden Gate Bridge to Muir Woods, named after the famous Scottish naturalist John Muir, to see the giant coastal redwoods (*Sequoia Sempervirens*). The trees, soaring up to 300ft. with a massive girth exceeding 30ft., were a fantastic sight. The bark is a lovely cinnamon, a rich light browny colour, quite rough and not dissimilar to a Cadbury's Flake. One dated back to 1,000BC which is absolutely amazing. The terrain was comparatively flat for pushing the wheelchair around, with a few steps in places but no real problems. It was a tranquil place, with lovely sunlight filtering through the trees. We drove back into the city over the Golden Gate Bridge.

Another day, we walked into the Chinatown district of San Francisco, which has a population of 64,000 people. It was a very interesting experience, seeing a different culture. We bought some fortune cookies there, which are sweet cookies, hollow inside with a paper message about your future, which was a bit of fun. Later we visited the Golden Gate Park, a large expanse of parkland, which incorporates the museum of natural history, which we enjoyed exploring. Unlike most museums this one has live exhibits: there were dolphins, porpoises and also crocodiles. We walked around the beautiful Japanese Tea Gardens, observing red wooden bridges, pagodas and the gorgeous array of oriental plants and flowers in their April full bloom.

The city of San Francisco is built on a hill, so it was quite hard going pushing a wheelchair around. Generally, it's not a very good place for wheelchairs!

From San Francisco we travelled to Monterey. After checking into an hotel for the night we drove onto Monterey's 17-mile drive. It was a lovely trip along the coast with picturesque scenery and beautiful white sandy beaches together with the Pacific Ocean. We saw a lot of seals on Seal Rock quite close to the shore of the Pacific, barking away. There were also many cypress trees on the drive, one in particular was called the Lone Pine Cypress. It was the highlight of the drive and much photographed on its coastal rocky outcrop, standing sentinel-like, guarding its coastal defences. Monterey has a nice fishermen's wharf, a small harbour and lot of old cannery buildings. We stopped off at a quaint little town called Carmel which had very expensive shops. There were quite a few steps about the place but there were no problems for me.

On a glorious hot sunny day we drove from Monterey down to Santa Barbara on Highway 1, which runs down the coast. Here the mountains drop down to the Pacific Ocean which sparkled like precious jewels in the sunlight. It is awesome scenic beauty with many hairpin bends – rather like Cornwall but on a bigger scale. I swam in the sea at Santa Barbara's Pacific Ocean coastline, a pleasant experience. It was whilst we were swimming that my sister Christine said, "Look there's a diver," but it was a harbour seal. Santa Barbara has over two miles of beaches and flat streets again making negotiating kerbs easier.

From Santa Barbara we drove back to Los Angeles to catch our flight home. As we had some time to kill, we decided to drive around Beverley Hills where many of the famous Hollywood stars live, together with other wealthy people. They had absolutely fabulous houses with beautiful gardens and pools.

After checking in at the airport we learned that our flight was delayed until the following day, so the airline put us up in the Cockatoo Inn overnight. We thought it should have been called the "Cock-up-atoo Inn"!

On the morning return flight there were no Jetways so my Dad had to lift me up the steps into the plane but there was no great difficulty. Dad also lifted another boy with Muscular Dystrophy onto the plane to help his mother.

On the return flight we had to refuel at Bangor in the State of Maine. A Jetway at this airport made access to the terminal building a great deal easier as we enjoyed the break, relaxing in the departure lounge. In one area the lounge had a tank full of huge Maine lobsters. An airport wheelchair was provided for me as my wheelchair was in the hold.

Arriving back at Gatwick there were no Jetways so Dad lifted me down the steps. Then we transferred to a mini bus which took us to the main terminal building. Just after I had taken a seat on the mini bus, I suddenly felt something pulling at my legs causing me to shout out in pain. Mum shrieked in warning also, as a man was pulling something from underneath my legs, which moments later we learned was a collapsible chair. It had become entangled with my legs and he was in danger of pulling them backwards with his efforts to remove the chair which was needed for the young person Dad had lifted on to the plane in Los Angeles. Thankfully, nothing was broken, and the man was very apologetic. Apart from this incident a fantastic holiday was had by all.

Chapter 5

Second Trip to America, April 1981
Florida, Alabama, Mississippi, Louisiana, Texas

This time when we travelled to America, we flew from London Heathrow Airport. I was now 14 years old. I had a bit of help at the airport to take me down to the plane. As usual, we had to be firm with the airport staff to make sure that the wheelchair went into the passenger part of the plane or in the hold and that it came out again at the next airport.

When we arrived at Miami International Airport we were met off the plane. I went into the airport wheelchair until my chair came out of the aircraft with the suitcases (not a very clever arrangement). The airport staff were most helpful. We had to go in a mini bus to collect our hire car for the holiday which meant I had to be lifted into the bus but there was no problem. I stayed in my wheelchair on the bus and Dad held the chair throughout. We picked the hire car up and drove north to Lauderdale-by-the-Sea, our base for a few days.

The first full day we visited the Everglades National Park which covers an area of a million square acres, where alligators live in their natural habitat. We travelled on an airboat around the Everglades which skimmed through sawgrass, crossed canals and went into lakes. At times the boat travelled at a rate of knots. This was an exhilarating experience. I had to be lifted onto the boat but there was no problem, although I needed holding onto, particularly when flying over the grasses.

30

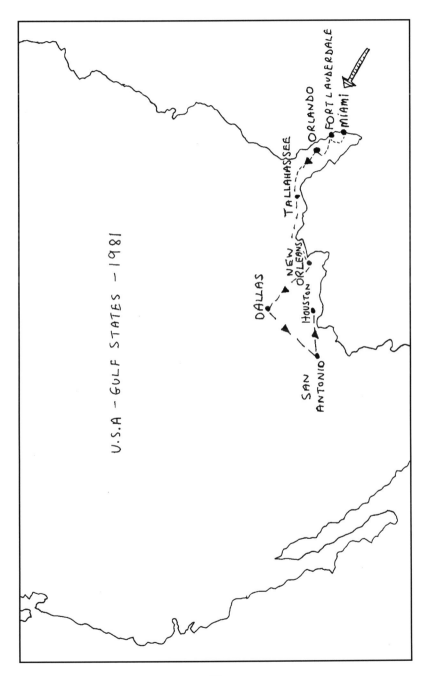

During the ride our guide pointed out to us a large alligator which was 17ft long. We spotted a few birds including a Great Blue Heron and a Purple Gallinule, a brightly coloured small bird.

During our stay in Lauderdale-by-the-Sea the first flight of the Space Shuttle *Columbia* blasted off from Cape Canaveral, Florida. We watched the coverage on the hotel room TV and took some slides from the television screen. Then we stepped outside the room for a few minutes and observed the vapour trail of the shuttle – it was a great sight. The space shuttle marked a major leap forward in spacecraft technology.

In Fort Lauderdale, at one restaurant, there were no steps to negotiate, which made it much easier to get in with my wheelchair. However, once inside, it was difficult to get my chair underneath the table because it was so low and it was hard for me to reach my food. From Lauderdale we drove north to Orlando where we had lunch at Arby's restaurant, which is famous for finely-sliced beef in a burger bun doused with horseradish relish fit to blow your brains out! We had steps to negotiate, which were no problem but once inside the restaurant we could not get my wheelchair close enough to the table, as a bar was in the way, so, with a bit of juggling with the footrests to avoid a table leg, and dangling my legs by the side of the footrests, I was able to get my chair under the table to feed myself.

The next day we visited the Kennedy Space Centre. We saw a lunar module and many spacecraft, including *Saturn V, Juno 1* and two other spaceships which were enormous, really amazing. There were a few steps about the place but they posed no great problems for us, because Dad was strong enough to negotiate with the wheelchair.

There was an excellent visitors' centre with many interesting exhibits. At the entrance, a guy dressed in spacesuit welcomed the visitors. We were able to see the Cape Canaveral launch pad in the distance.

Later that day we travelled on to the town of Daytona Beach, famous for NASCAR (National Association of Stock Car Auto Racing) events where souped-up saloon-type cars race around at speeds over 200mph on a bevelled track. Nearby was Daytona Beach itself which stretches some miles along the Atlantic seaboard. Lots of cars, motor bikes and way-out machines race up and down the beach. It was here at Daytona Beach that Malcolm Campbell broke the land speed record in his car *Bluebird* in 1931.

We returned to our base in Orlando in the late afternoon.

Another day we visited the huge theme park aquarium called Sea World in Orlando; it is home to Shamu the killer whale and other creatures like walrus, dolphins, otters and flamingos. In another part of the Park it was possible to encounter sharks by taking a conveyor belt through a glass tunnel – it was quite an experience seeing the sharks surrounding you!

Then we travelled from Orlando to Tallahassee, the State capital of Florida in the northern part of the State. We walked around the old and new parts of the town and went into the ultra-modern capitol building which was very interesting. The pavements were comparatively flat with ramps in places; there were a few kerbs to negotiate but no real problems.

From Tallahassee we drove to New Orleans, a distance of approximately 400-plus miles, travelling through two States, Alabama and Mississippi.

We stopped off at Pensacola Beach where the sand was white. I have never seen sand so white, it was just like snow.

As we drew near to New Orleans we went over many bridges and causeways over lakes, inland waterways and swamps, known as 'bayous'. We stayed in New Orleans a few nights.

New Orleans is known as the Paris of America and the jazz

capital of the world. We walked around the famous French quarter of the city including Jackson Square and Bourbon Street. The buildings here had beautiful wrought iron balconies and lovely flower-filled patios. As we walked down Bourbon Street in the evening when it was lit up, there were lots of people tap-dancing in the street and the sound of jazz music could be heard echoing from the restaurants, creating a fabulous atmosphere. There were quite a lot of high kerbs about the place with more ramps in the newer parts of New Orleans.

Another day we took a trip on the Mississippi River on a paddle steamer called the *Natchez*, built in 1976. The voyage took a few hours. There was a ramp onto the steamer which made it a lot easier for the wheelchair. There were a few steps to negotiate in order to move around the *Natchez*, but there were no difficulties. We strolled to the stern of the boat to observe the enormous paddles which propelled it. At 2,348 miles the Mississippi is the longest river in the United States of America and is also the third longest river in the world.

We drove from New Orleans to Dallas, which is approximately 500 miles, the longest journey of the holiday. We passed the Superdrome Sports Stadium on the way out of New Orleans – the largest sports stadium in the world. It is a fantastic high-tech building and home to the New Orleans football team, the Saints.

In Dallas we saw the book repository building from where Lee Harvey Oswald shot John. F. Kennedy in 1963 and visited the John F. Kennedy Museum, which was very moving. Outside Dallas there are some fantastic ranches and houses. One we saw was the South Fork Ranch, which was used in the T.V. series *Dallas*. We drove from Dallas to San Antonio and stopped off at the State capital of Texas, Austin, where we saw the splendid rotunda dome of the capitol building. San Antonio is where the Battle of the Alamo took place in 1836 and there is a mission there called the Alamo. The battle of the

Alamo was fought by a handful of Texan men, including Davy Crockett and Jim Bowie. They held up the Mexican Army at the Alamo; as a result of this action General Sam Houston and his army were able to defeat the Mexicans at the battle of San Jacinto and so gained independence for Texas. Davy Crockett is known as the "King of the Wild West Frontier".

While I was in San Antonio we chatted to a policemen by the name of J Leal, and I asked him about the gun he carried. It was a Magnum and he brought it out of his holster together with the bullets for me to look at. He went on to explain that all police officers in the U.S.A. are issued with the Magnum, an advantage being that in tight situations, 'ammo' can be shared. I had quite a long chat with this policeman – he was a very friendly chap.

From San Antonio we travelled on to Houston where we visited an absolutely enormous shopping complex called the Galleria with floors and floors of beautiful shops, some of which were very exclusive. There was a lift in the Galleria which was made almost entirely from glass and no steps at all, which made pushing the wheelchair very easy. The Galleria also had an ice rink in the middle of the complex. While we were in there a tornado hit downtown Houston and blew the roof off a building.

Also in Houston we drove past the famous Astrodome Sports Stadium, which is huge, but not as large, however, as the New Orleans Superdome.

For the return flight home we flew out of Houston International Airport. There was a Jetway to help board the plane and as I reached the threshold of the plane I was put into a wheelchair-like trolley and wheeled down the aisle of the plane until I reached my seat, which was a great help. My own wheelchair went into the hold of the plane. The plane had to refuel at J.F.K. Airport in New York and whilst this was being done I went into the airport's own wheelchair. Once the plane was re-fuelled and we were back on board we taxied onto the runway to join a queue of 20 other aircraft waiting to take off.

There was a Jetway at Heathrow Airport, and I went into an airport wheelchair until mine came off the plane with the suitcases.

Chapter 6

Back operation, 1982

Within a month of our move back in Chester from the Fylde in August 1982, when I was 15, an appointment was made for me to attend the clinic at the Robert Jones and Agnes Hunt Hospital, Gabowen, to sort out various things like wheelchairs and general care. The doctors then talked about having a spinal fusion operation, which came as a shock to us. At this time I had, since moving to Chester, attended Dorin Park special school in Upton-by-Chester for about two weeks. I was transported each day in an ambulance. Ten days later I was in hospital being prepared for spinal surgery. Respiratory functions tests were carried out and lots of other breathing exercises to improve my breathing. There was a great concern about my lung capacity, but after many tests it was decided to go ahead with the operation which took place on a very sunny, crisp September morning. Before I had the operation the curvature of my spine was 60 degrees. I decided that I wanted the operation from the beginning, but my parents were not sure about it. It was a difficult decision to make. The night before the operation my Dad was still undecided and after much talking I said, "If I don't have the operation I will keep on about it." I was upset that Dad wouldn't sign the consent form for me to have the operation, so I stormed off to the day room and left him behind. Later on that night Dad signed the form, which I was extremely pleased about. I was never apprehensive about having the operation.

After the operation the curvature of my spine was 12 degrees. When I came round I remember saying to the Sister: "Have they performed the operation?" as I couldn't believe it had been done. I was in a bit of a daze, which was to be expected. I looked around my surroundings and saw the intravenous drip dripping away. I was in intensive care for 24 hours. Shortly after the operation I had my back X-rayed which was very uncomfortable, then I realised the operation had been performed. Twenty-four hours later I was lifted into my wheelchair which was painful on my hips   which you can imagine if your back has been straightened up. You see, the procedure involved taking scrapings of bone from my pelvic area which were then transferred and sprinkled on my back to encourage new bone growth on my spine. I am told the bone has now formed like a sheet. Each day after my operation I sat in my chair for longer periods of time till eventually I could sit in it all day without pain. Sometimes during the day I rested on my bed.

A few days after the operation my Dad tried to lift me, but he didn't have the confidence and didn't want to hurt me. Professor Edwards came to see me and was delighted that everything had gone perfectly well. I had to wait for two months to be fitted with a new electric chair but the hospital provided a makeshift chair in the meantime. The main advantage of the operation was that I could sit a lot straighter in my wheelchair, and with a straight back it is easier to fight off chest infections because the lungs are not inhibited, therefore making breathing easier. When I came home from the hospital I was perfectly straight; I hardly moved at all going round sharp corners and could balance better in the car than before. The operation helps posture immensely, for when your back is bent all the time your organs get squashed and digestion is more difficult.

I wasn't able to sit up in bed until about six months after the operation, as my hips ached a lot. I was not able to bend forward as much as I used to without hurting myself.

Following the operation I was at home, off school, for about six weeks, then in November 1982 I started back once again. I was there for two weeks and picked up a nasty chest infection, which took about a month to clear. Half way through the chest infection I went for a routine check-up to University College Hospital, London. As soon as I arrived in the hospital I had a chest X-ray and some intensive physiotherapy. I stayed in the hospital for a further week until my chest infection had completely cleared. Whilst I was in the hospital the Princess of Wales opened a maternity wing for premature babies and I was taken by one of the nurses to see her. Princess Diana chatted to us and told us she had just seen some very tiny babies. Whilst I was in the hospital I did quite a lot of drawing, lots of sketches and cartoons to occupy my time. After the chest infection my parents and I decided that it was too cold during the winter to go to school and risk a severe cold, and so I continued my learning at home with work sent from Dorin Park School.

In December 1982 I got a new Vessa electric wheelchair. The seat sagged so my Dad inserted a piece of wood into it which helped a lot, but sometimes the wood slipped to one side and made it more difficult to balance, consequently I fell to one side which was a bit frustrating. Our house has a large garden where I used to roam, using my wheelchair. The gravel paths around it posed a problem particularly when the wheels of the electric wheelchair became bogged down which was annoying and made me skid the chair with some frustration close to anger. Sometimes I was able to redeem myself but at other times I needed assistance.

Developing new skills and time occupation
Whilst on home leave from school I spent most days designing Christmas and birthday cards and by the end of 1983 had completed over 200 birthday cards of various designs, for

example, using cartoon characters and floral designs. This work became a little monotonous after a time so I had the bright idea of designing a Christmas card and having it printed, which was a great success. The first card was a design based on the famous Chester clock in Foregate Street.

In September 1983 I resumed an earlier interest of painting on stones picked up from the beach. Beginning with simple designs such as daisies, cats and fish, I then graduated onto animals and birds, becoming more skilled with practice. As time went on I found I could paint almost anything, especially birds. Friends also commissioned me to paint their dogs. These pictures were done on paper using gouache, which turned out well and the friends were very pleased with them. Subsequent designs for cards also followed and featured an owl, printed as a notelet, a church scene for Christmas, and a robin, also for Christmas. At the time of writing the kingfisher shown on one of the colour pages is featured on a card which is sold in aid of Muscular Dystrophy, Cancer Research and Christian charities.

In 1988 I painted my last stone because my strength became insufficient to lift and coordinate the apparatus of painting. When I realised that I could no longer paint I wasn't down about the circumstance – I was pleased to have had the ability to pursue this occupation. "God never closes a door without opening the window of opportunity to something better." An encouraging thought. At this juncture I had sold over 200 stones/slates and 5,000 cards. My favourite slate was a European eagle owl which I could have sold many times. I enjoyed painting and found it a challenge.

Towards the end of 1990 I turned my attention to developing an earlier interest in pen and ink drawings, only this time drawing mainly mountainscapes and animals. Before attempting this medium with pen and ink, I did not think I would have the strength to draw. I was pleased that I could even though I was limited working with drawing movements within

Left: My kingfisher card has been used by various charities;

Below right: a swallow painted on stone.

Above: rhino painted on slate;

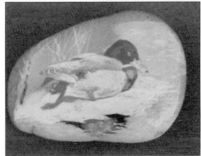

right: mallard painted on stone;

below: bull painted on slate.

a 25mm x 25mm area. To go to a different area someone had to move my hand and re-position the pen.

I spend a lot of time reading and watching various wildlife and many travel videos. I also have friends who pop in from time to time for a chat. In addition to these activities another pastime I enjoy is listening to music. I am quite catholic in my taste and range from classical to pop and heavy rock. I also take an interest in sport, particularly football (for my sins my team is Liverpool), tennis, rugby and Formula 1 motor racing, to name but a few.

In 1984 January a contact was made with an education officer who was very helpful to me, he thought it would be a good idea to go back to Hebden Green special school. I went three days a week to study geography and biology. I started back at Hebden Green about April, and Mum used to take me in the van. Towards the end of 1984 I found it increasingly difficult to feed myself – it strained my stomach leaning forwards and obviously my food got cold in the meantime.

Sometimes I found balancing difficult in my wheelchair; I got frustrated and annoyed. However most of the time I accepted the fact. When I was being lifted into the car, I felt uncomfortable at times, and I asked myself if had I got the confidence to be lifted. Mum and Dad were concerned not to trap my legs or arms and there was the possibility of Mum or Dad hurting their backs. However, when I stayed with my aunt and uncle, I got concerned when they lifted me; at the time I would think to myself, "Will they knock my body or lift me high enough up, will they hurt their backs or injure themselves?" I became a little anxious when other people pushed my chair who were not used to it, thinking to myself, "Will they tip my chair up when I go down kerbs or what will they do if the pavement is not smooth?" It was up to me to remind them what to do.

Chapter 7

South of France Holiday, July 1983
Cote d'Azur

On this holiday, when I was 16, we flew to Nice from Manchester. I received a bit of help to board the plane at the airport to transfer from my wheelchair, which, in the absence of a Jetway, was at the base of the steps ready to be carried into the Boeing 727. As always, we were firm with the airport officials to make sure my wheelchair was stowed in the aircraft's hold, but not before we had removed the headrest to save it being lost. During the flight we flew over the snow-capped French Alps. Upon arriving at Nice airport I had to make sure the wheelchair came off before it was taken off with the luggage. Although an airport wheelchair could be made available, it was unsuitable for my needs as it lacked a head-rest.

Nice was our base in the South of France. Our hotel room overlooked the beach and the crystal-clear waters of the Mediterranean. A short stroll from the hotel was the Promenade des Anglais, a long palm-tree lined road with flat surfaces along the sea front. Off the *promenade* a ramp led onto the pebble beach and then to a short concrete path leading to a larger area of concrete for disabled people not too far from the water's edge, which was ideal for me to dress and undress. This made visiting the beach very easy and there was a special chair provided with large inflatable wheels in the shape of footballs, which if needed could go into the sea – but my Dad lifted me in because, again, there was no headrest available.

In the newer part of Nice there were many modern shops and a Galleria-type shopping complex called the Nice Etoile, with many interesting shops. In the shopping complex there was also a glass lift. The whole area was air-conditioned, a refreshing change in the heat and a bonus since our hotel didn't have a system. The old part of the town was particularly beautiful, with many attractive buildings and churches down quaint narrow streets

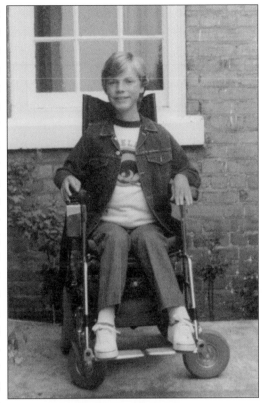

Me aged 16, pictured at home

with a nice atmosphere. There were huge fountains, some classical, some modern, and a particularly impressive one at a roundabout, comprising a group of figures. The spray from it gave off a nice cooling effect in the intense heat of the day.

One night, in the old part of the town, I had a fabulous fish meal, beginning with fish soup and followed by squid marinated in cognac – delicious! I adore my sea food diet. I see food and eat it!! (Forgive the pun!)

From Nice we visited the Principality of Monaco which is separated from France by an invisible border. On our journey there we travelled along the coast road high above the ocean and from this vantage point we saw many attractive beaches. The coastline was comparatively rugged and from the road we could also see lots of beautiful houses and apartments. We drove on until we were near to Prince Rainier's Palace high on a cliff-top. We parked the car before walking to a lift in order to get fairly close to the Palace area at the cliff face. It was not too far to push the chair, just a slight hill to negotiate and then a flight of stairs, but no real difficulties.

There was plenty of lush greenery to see and exotic Mediterranean flowers in full bloom. The streets closer to the Palace were quaint, with cobblestones in places; it was quite a bumpy ride for me in the wheelchair but there were no problems. Just as we arrived the changing of the guards procession at Rainier's Palace was taking place – perfect timing! The guards had smart white uniforms with gold braiding.

As we drove along the front at Monaco we observed a large marina with all the fantastic speed boats and other ocean-going craft. The Mediterranean was a beautiful azure blue in the sunshine – a marked contrast to the majority of the buildings with their orange and brown roofs and sandstone walls.

From Monaco we travelled on to Menton, a town near the Italian border with a pleasant marina and a long stretch of sandy beach, flat pavements, no ramps but only medium sized kerbs that caused us few problems. There were many fruit stalls on the roadside selling mouth-watering melons.

In Italy we visited Bordighera, which is famous for its sun-bathing resorts and is regarded as one of the best on the Riviera. We travelled back to Nice on the Cornice road high up in the hills, which provided some brilliant views of the sea and towns along the way.

On another day trip from Nice, we went to Cannes. On the way we travelled through Antibes and saw the remains of the old castle. There are many sandy beaches between Antibes and Juan les Pins.

We stopped off at Juan les Pins which is known as a health resort. It was at this point Dad realised he had left his swimming trunks behind in the hotel in Nice and so decided, as we wanted to swim at Cannes, to purchase a new pair. They turned out to be the most expensive pair he ever bought! We walked around the town of Juan les Pins for a while. It had medium sized kerbs with nice flat pavements and the odd ramps.

Cannes is a famous resort with some beautiful hotels such as the Carlton, and is noted for its yearly film festival. I had a swim there. There was a ramp provided to get onto the beach which was absolutely packed. Dad had to lift me across the crowds – it was a bit like a maze. After my swim when Dad was getting me dressed, people kept staring, which prompted me to say to the family, "You would think they had never seen anyone being dressed before in Cannes!" – considering the number of naked bodies around the place.

From Cannes we drove into the hills to Grasse, the scent capital of the world, to visit a perfumery. The scenery was attractive with lots of greenery. We saw many beautiful properties with red and orange roofs and attractive arches. There are fields upon fields of lavender which is grown for the perfume industry. It was interesting to visit the perfumery.

An aside: *The women in France smell like a Perfumery and the men smell like a Puffumery...*

We had a super holiday. At the airport in Nice we had to make sure once again, that the wheelchair went into the hold. We were met at Manchester by an airport official. Dad lifted me down the steps of the plane straight into my wheelchair and then off into the sunset we headed!

In 1983 an opportunity arose to purchase a specially adapted Renault Trafic van which was equipped with a side ramp and anchor points in the floor to which the wheelchair could be securely clamped. The van was a green, a colour which gave rise to it being dubbed, "the Green Goddess". This mean machine gave me a new lease of life in that it allowed me to become more independent in a number of ways. Firstly, the amount of 'man-handling' was reduced dramatically as I could drive the wheelchair straight in to the clamping position. Once in I could be taken to places and deployed into the surrounding territory and then collected. Sorties into Chester and its environs became a regular feature, plus magical mystery tours into Wales. Of course someone always accompanied me, but even so such outings were very liberating! The height of the van gave me a new perspective on the world around, seeing things not possible from the car. The van served us well for a number of years until the spring of 1990 at which time the quality of the air I breathed became a more important factor – if it was too hot it made me breathless, if it was too cold it was just not comfortable for me. The problem was solved by the more modern air conditioning system in our car. By the time we came to part company with the Green Goddess van we had clocked up a considerable number of miles and travelled far and wide!

Chapter 8

Physiotherapy

Physiotherapy is extremely important for Muscular Dystrophy sufferers. One day in 1984, talking to the physiotherapist at Hebden Green, Miss Pat Bennett, I asked if she would agree that the five principal exercises are:-

1. Standing in a swivel walker
2. Swimming
3. Flowtron machine
4. Stretching of limbs
5. Breathing exercises

When I stood up in the standing frame after six years in a wheelchair I was absolutely amazed. I didn't think I could stand again: it was a little painful and feeling the blood pumping all over my body was an exhilarating experience. I felt a little light-headed being in an upright position. I thought it would have been more painful. However, when I first stood in a swivel walker my legs, hips and ankles were quite bent. I had three-and-a-half inch thick wedged blocks under my feet when the walker was first delivered. After a couple of months my wedges were altered to one inch.

Incidentally, I could only stand up in the swivel walker with the aid of special boots and wearing callipers. Standing up in a swivel walker is the most important single exercise for it helps blood flow and general circulation, it also limits aches and pains when you are sitting in your wheelchair. Once, having done these exercises, I found I slept better and did not wake up

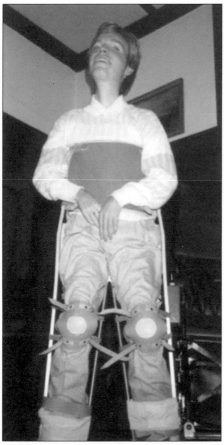

Me in my walker, aged 18

as much. The swivel walker is an absolutely fantastic invention; it can be painful sometimes and your legs generally ache each time you stand up, but you have to experience a certain amount of discomfort, it helps in the end, as long as it is not too uncomfortable. Standing is good for the heart and lungs, it loosens the tissues of the body, and helps with kidney and bladder drainage. When sitting, the bones of the body are more brittle and the calcium levels are lower.

Another brilliant standing device is called the Levo stand-up wheelchair. There are two versions of this, one is the push chair and the other is an electric version. I have tried the electric Levo wheelchair and it is excellent.

One evening at home my Mum and Dad put me in my walker. I was walking on the carpet, and then I lost balance because of the thickness of the carpet. As I started to fall I couldn't shout out as I was speechless from the shock of falling. My Dad and sister were in the room at the time and didn't realise, until I was two feet from the ground. At that moment Mum walked into the room and dived and tried to stop me, she made the speed of the fall slower. I knocked my head on the fireplace but wasn't hurt badly, just a small cut and I felt fine after a short time. Coincidentally, after the fall I discovered the foot plates were too short; soon afterwards they were replaced and it was a lot safer. It rocked my confidence for a while but it soon returned. After about six months of practising walking I walked over 20 metres. Then after standing for a few months my legs and hips were not too far off full extension. Each evening before I went to bed Mum and Dad generally did my exercises by bending and stretching my limbs.

At this time, on occasions when I had a cold or chest infection postural drainage had to be applied. This now has to be done several times a day. It involves lying horizontally and tilted back slightly and then being slapped with cupped hands across the chest before being turned onto both sides in turn, for the same treatment. The idea is to dislodge phlegm, help bring it up and so improve breathing.

It was suggested in 1975 that I should have the tendons cut in my feet, as this would ensure that they would be straight and not curve in during later years. I decided against this because I didn't particularly want another operation and I thought it was purely cosmetic. With good physiotherapy my feet are not so bad – they have curved in over the years with no serious consequences, although in recent years my toe-nails are not "a pretty sight", probably due to poor circulation. I use anti-fungal cream to soften the nails and hopefully they eventually drop off. One nail has already reached this stage and a new nail is now forming.

Chapter 9

A Girlfriend

In 1984 at Hebden School I had a girlfriend named Katherine who had Spina Bifida. When I first set eyes on her, I didn't have enough courage to chat to her because I was nervous, my heart kept beating faster and faster. I heard somebody mentioning her name, and I was sure they said Katherine. A few days later I chatted to her friend to make sure her name was Katherine. She said it was and asked me why I wanted to know, so I said, "because I like her!"

The following day I talked to Katherine and my words came out fast because I was nervous. I found out that she was studying three A Levels and three extra 0 Levels. Two of her A Levels were in French and German, and she studied at the comprehensive school next door to Hebden School called Woodford Lodge. Katherine came back from school next door most school breaktimes. Although she attended Woodford Lodge, she was still attached to Hebden Green. Katherine talked about her driving lessons. At the time she drove a Mini Metro which had been specially adapted with hand controls. Incidentally, her parents had to buy the car before she took any driving lessons.

Approximately a week later Katherine passed her test. I chatted to her on a number of occasions in school, and on my 17th birthday I asked her out. I just couldn't believe it when she said yes! The following Saturday afternoon Katherine came to my house in her car. It was a beautiful sunny day when she first arrived and I took her down the garden to see the menagerie – our sheep, lambs and ducks. All our sheep had names, one of the lambs was an orphan called Benji. We went on a two-mile walk around the country lanes and had to be very careful because of cars travelling fast round the lanes – my electric chair is quite noisy and this makes it difficult to hear cars coming. We chatted away and enjoyed ourselves in the blazing sunshine. She gave me a demonstration of how fast she could propel herself – amazingly quickly!

A month later I took Katherine out for lunch. Mum took us in our van and dropped us both off in Chester. Katherine went up the ramp of the van and transferred onto one of the seats. Her wheelchair went at the side of her. Then I drove up the ramp and into my clamping position. Before having lunch Katherine took my belt off so that I could feed myself more easily. She also cut up my food which was a great help.

Seven weeks later we finished going out together, but remained good friends. We chatted to each other in the school corridors, but not as much as we used to. On 1st August I invited Katherine to my house and we both went on a three-mile walk in the countryside nearby. I found it quite difficult balancing in my chair at times when the road cambered off and Katherine found it slightly difficult. After the walk we listened to music, love songs. Katherine went through the alphabet in German with me which was good fun. Before she came to my house the family and I had just returned from a holiday in Europe, a few days before (see next chapter). We had spent a day in Germany.

Katherine flew on holiday to Jersey with her friend, who was also in a wheelchair. Soon after she returned from holiday I was invited to her house. It was a beautiful sunny day again and we went for a walk in the countryside. There was a stream and a field with two fabulous horses. The summer colours looked beautiful in one part of the lane where the trees covered it, forming an arch. It was so tranquil. Katherine asked me to go back out with her. I said yes, she missed me and I missed her while she was on holiday. Absence does makes the heart grow fonder. Then I invited Katherine to my house again and we went on a long walk but it began to rain, it got heavier and heavier and we sheltered under a tree – laughter in the rain! My Mum decided to come out in the van to look for us because of the rain. She found us both and off we went home in the van, we were a bit wet but soon dried out by the home comforts of the fire.

As you can imagine, kissing somebody in a wheelchair is quite difficult. Katherine took my belt off my chair, then parked her chair alongside mine until she was in the correct position. She lifted my hands up and put them round her neck, then she had to wait until my hands were balanced and hold me so that I wouldn't fall forwards.

In September Katherine flew off to West Germany to a rehabilitation centre on her own to improve her German. She sent me a postcard written in German, so I got my friend to read it to me. Katherine liked sport and played basketball and archery. The school started a basketball team, and Katherine had also taken part in the Stoke Mandeville games on a number of occasions with Hebden Green School.

Towards the end of September Katherine finished going out with me, but we remained good friends. She boosted my ego and I felt more confident in myself. I will never forget her: she will have a special place in my heart.

Chapter 10

European Holiday, July 1984

Belgium, Germany, Holland

Travelling arrangements for this holiday – when I was 17 – were originally made for the cross-Channel ferry, from Dover. However, about nine days before we were due to travel, the workers at the terminal went on strike. Because of these circumstances about five days prior to leaving we decided to catch a plane, flying from Heathrow airport. It was good to have a Jetway to the plane. The flight time to Brussels was 45 minutes.

After checking in at our hotel we walked down town for an evening meal which we ate "alfresco" in a narrow side street. I enjoyed a Lasagne as the evening lights came up adding to the ambience of the moment. It is said that there are more restaurants in Brussels per head of the population than in Paris.

The following day we walked for miles around the city of Brussels. We saw many interesting buildings and landmarks, including a monument with an everlasting flame at the base of it, the Justice courts, Brussels Palace and the Grand Place. The Grand Place is a square in one of the oldest parts of Brussels. One building in particular, the town hall, dates back to the 13th century. The buildings which dominate the other three sides of the square bear dates from the 17th century and were commissioned by and for the major Guilds of the day, such as the Brewers, the Lacemakers, the Stonemasons. These Guildhalls

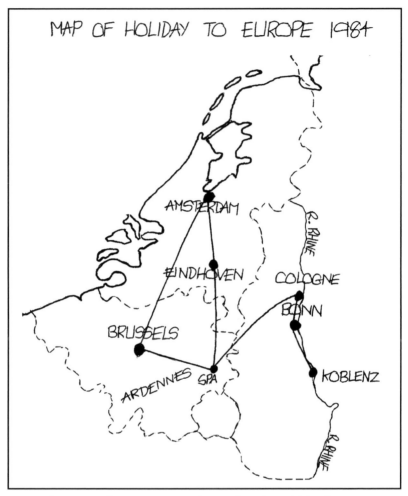

MAP OF HOLIDAY TO EUROPE 1984

AMSTERDAM

EINDHOVEN

COLOGNE

R. RHINE

BONN

BRUSSELS

ARDENNES SPA

KOBLENZ

R. RHINE

are architecturally stunning, adorned with gold leaf, numerous coats of arms and I found them ornate but pleasing to look at. They have a lot of character and style. In the older parts of Brussels there were cobblestones all over the place which made it difficult pushing the chair around, very bumpy – I was shaken but not stirred – but we made it!

In Brussels I watched a lady lace-making in one of the arcades, this is an old but famous craft of Brussels. We walked around a lot of attractive side streets with cafés and restaurants which had umbrellas over the tables. In another part of town we saw the famous Mannequin Piss, a statuette of a small boy weeing at passers-by. We visited a large park on the outskirts of Brussels in which there is a building called the "Atomium". This landmark was built for the World Fair of 1958. In the Park it was fairly flat ground for pushing the wheelchair.

We travelled out of Brussels to the spa-town of Spa in the Belgian Ardennes, which is a skiing resort in the winter months. On our way we passed through lush greenery and some lovely rural villages. We stayed high up in the Ardennes just outside Spa, where our hotel room had a balcony which overlooked the picturesque Ardennes with its hilly forests and a beautiful lake.

Later that day we drove into Spa, a pretty little place with a large casino. Once a year a Formula 1 Grand Prix event is held there.

We crossed the Belgian border into the Republic of West Germany. Our first stop-off was Cologne, a lovely city with attractive buildings. The famous cathedral, which remained untouched during World War Two bombing raids, dominated the skyline. It's an impressive edifice with a very pointed spire and beautiful stained glass windows. We stopped for refreshments at a café overlooking the cathedral. The part of Cologne which we walked around had flat ground for pushing the wheelchair, in places there were ramps and a number of kerbs to bump up and down but no difficulty. We picked up a number of enormous Frankfurter sausages which we took out and scoffed down at a suitable location nearby!

We travelled from Cologne to nearby Bonn, the capital of West Germany. Like Cologne, Bonn is on the River Rhine. We didn't stop off there owing to our time schedule, but drove around to take in the sights. Motoring from Bonn we followed the course of the River Rhine valley. The river is very wide in

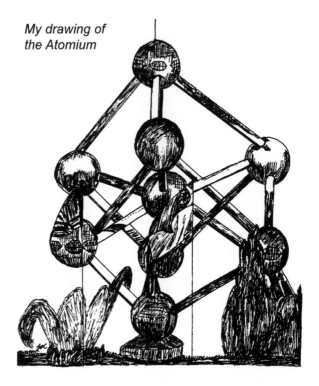

*My drawing of
the Atomium*

parts and a lot of elongated barges travel down it with their
cargoes. Many families live on these barges and some people
transport their cars on deck. We stopped off at a quaint village
called Remagen where the British Army blew up the bridge
over the Rhine during the Second World War. The mission was
made into a film called *A Bridge too Far*, some years ago. In
Remagen we saw some beautiful Tudor style houses with lovely flowers in the window boxes. Then we continued driving
further down the Rhine to Koblenz. One of the buildings
looked Russian in style with its "onion dome". From Koblenz
we travelled back to Spa and saw the Moselle River which
flows into the Rhine. The River Rhine valley is a famous wine
growing and producing region of the world. Tobacco and
wheat are also grown on the steep hilly slopes. It is a pictur-

esque area. On our car journey down the Rhine Valley we saw some lovely castles guarding the river.

From Spa we went to Eindhoven, a very modern city in Holland. On the way we saw the River Meuse which flows through Belgium and as we travelled through Holland we saw a lot of farmland and many attractive windmills. Later that day, after checking into our hotel and having had a light lunch, we walked around Eindhoven which had flat pavements and ramps with a few high kerbs to tackle, no problem!

The following day we went on an excursion in the car from Eindhoven to Amsterdam and saw many avenues of trees on either side of the roads. Much of Holland is below sea level and because of this the land can easily flood; that is why there are dykes to stop water from encroaching, therefore preventing crops from being ruined and the houses and windmills from being damaged too. We saw lots of windmills and a number of wind-powered generators, resembling huge propellers, erected to provide electricity.

Upon arriving in Amsterdam we took a boat trip around the labyrinth of canals. Along the canals there are said to be 2,000 houseboats and 1,203 bridges – which is staggering! We saw lots of super buildings including churches and merchants' houses – one particular building dated back to the Renaissance period. One canal was called the Gentleman's Canal. Part of the boat trip took us out of the canal system for a short time into a major waterway large enough to accommodate sea-going vessels, for example, tankers delivering crude oil to the Shell refinery there. In the distance we could see the Maritime Museum with some large rigged sailing ships. After an enjoyable sail, in Amsterdam's famous enclosed glass boats, we strolled around the city and saw lots of old and modern shops. The pavements were comparatively flat, with a few cracks in places and occasional ramps with fairly low kerbs. There was a tram system running through the town. I remember having a light meal down a side street, sitting outside and sampling the Dutch beer. It was shortly afterwards that nature called and I was glad to urinate into my bottle rather than entering the humiliating circular cast iron public urinals which left little to the imagination for the passers-by. That evening we had a fabulous meal in our hotel, the Van der Valk; the entrée was a succulent *Weiner Schienitzel*, which is veal with ham and cheese, the lot wrapped in bread crumbs. The hotel menu was amazing, and the restaurant was full every night. We also saw a large tank full of live lobsters.

The following day on the journey back to Brussels to fly home, we passed many coal mines. Coal mining is an important industry in Belgium but coal deposits have declined because of alternative energy resources. Once on board and since there was a delay for take off, I was invited into the cockpit of the plane and it was very interesting to learn about different aspects of the aircraft. We had to circle around once over London because of the air traffic – it was a clear day and we had an excellent view of Metropolitan London sights including Buckingham Palace. A great week's holiday!

Chapter 11

Third Trip to America, June 1985

Connecticut, New York, Massachusetts, Rhode Island, New Jersey, Maryland, Virginia, Pennsylvania

I was 18 this time when I visited America in June 1985. I had a wheelchair with a high headrest so we had to make sure it was stored in the passenger part of the plane. I had a bit of help to board the plane and we were met off it at J.F.K. airport.

On the first day in America we visited Greenwich, Connecticut. The area was particularly beautiful, with lovely houses, lush greenery and a park with a tranquil lake. In another part there was a huge marina with a small sandy beach with access to the Atlantic Ocean. Most of the buildings were made from wood – a typical building material for the American style of housing. We stopped off in nearby Riverside to get doughnuts from "Dunkin Donuts," the flavours included doughnuts with maple icing poured on top and Boston Creams, which were covered in chocolate and filled with naughty-but-nice custard, delicious!

Our next destination was New York City, known as "The Big Apple." As we drew near to New York the highway branched out into twelve lanes – it was very busy. There are toll roads here which meant chucking the cash for the toll into a tub before using the road. We saw all the skyscrapers in the gleaming sunshine as we approached New York where we stayed on 51st Street, 7th Avenue at the Sheraton City Squire. That after-

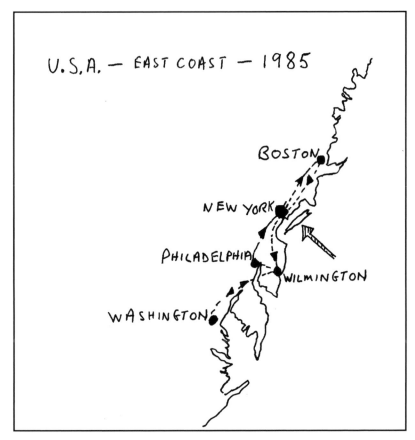

noon we walked around the Rockerfeller Centre and Broadway, Time Square. The kerbs were steep and there were hardly any ramps to use, but there were few problems because Dad was strong enough to negotiate with the wheelchair. We then went up the Empire State Building (1,472ft high) which stands in the heart of Manhattan on 5th Avenue and 34th Street. The building was opened on 1st May 1931. After ascending in the elevator we had to go up a number of steps to reach the observatory on the 102nd floor of the building but there was no difficulty because Dad could bump the chair up and down the steps. It was a good thing for him that I was lightweight...

The vista of New York was fantastic and the height of the Empire State Building amazed me. Incidentally, it was the tallest building in the world until the Twin Towers of the World Trade Centre were built in Manhattan. The Twin Towers then held the record until the Sears Tower was built in Chicago. Sadly, everyone knows what subsequently happened to the World Trade Centre on 11th September 2001.

While we were in New York we went on the Circle Line cruise around Manhattan island, regarded as America's favourite boat trip. There was a ramp onto the boat then a flight of steps to get up on to the top deck, but no problem. There were many landmarks and places of interest to see on the trip such as the Statue of Liberty on Liberty Island, Gracie Mansion, the home of the Mayor of New York, the Twin Towers, and Ellis Island, which was known as immigrants' island and the first port of call before immigrants were permitted to land in the USA. Sometimes, they might have to wait several weeks before being allowed entry. We also sailed by Governors Island and the Palisades, which are Schist rock formations, and the famous George Washington Bridge. It was a brilliant way to see New York in three hours! To disembark I had a bit of help going down the steps.

Later on that day we walked into Central Park and saw a bird which Dad thought was a jay, but I later asked a friend, "What is the bird which looks like a jay and is blue?" The reply came back, "It's a Blue Jay!"

From New York we drove to Boston, Massachusetts, travelling through the State of Connecticut. Boston stands on the Charles River. While we were in Boston we visited a huge food market called Quincy Market, in Faneuil Hall marketplace. There were stalls and shops displaying food from all over the world, flowers, boutiques and lots of fancy goods and beautiful cakes. We had a coffee there, which was very welcome seeing as though the day was particularly cold. I had a delicious "Swan cake," made largely from meringue filled with cream. There were ramps inside the market with flat pavements which made it easier pushing the wheelchair.

It was in Boston that I saw Paul Revere's house. Paul Revere was an express horse rider, and was involved in the Boston Tea Party, when tons of tea imported from the East Indian Tea Company were dumped into the harbour by the Bostonians in protest against the British. Paul Revere made his famous ride in 1775 when he rode to Lexington to warn the Americans about the attack by the British Army. We strolled back to Quincy Market and waited a long time for a taxi back to the hotel in the freezing cold weather. While journeying back to our hotel in the taxi we saw more of the city of Boston observing rows of town houses which had architectural character, each front door possessing a flight of steps with iron handrail. We had dinner later at a famous seafood restaurant which was in our hotel complex; there were a few steps to tackle but no problem. My wheelchair fitted right underneath the table so eating was no problem at all. For my entrée that night I had Shrod Fish.

The following day we drove to Plymouth, a quaint little town with a small marina with quite a lot of fishing boats. It was here we saw a replica of *Mayflower II* which brought the Pilgrim Fathers (English Puritans) to land in Plymouth in 1620. We observed a rock where they landed, called "Plymouth Rock," inscribed with the date of their arrival. The whole rock is enclosed within a Greek style structure of open columns supporting the roof canopy. There are a lot of beautiful houses and gardens outside the main town of Plymouth, with picturesque vistas. We saw the Plymouth plantation, a living museum where people live and work as they did at the time of the Pilgrim Fathers, but did not have enough time to look around.

We then drove onto the 90-mile long Cape Cod peninsula as

far as Hyannis, a nice place with a fairly large marina. We drove back to Boston from Hyannis and met Pauline and Derek, more friends of ours, in the hotel bar, where we had a good chat and a laugh. Derek was there for six months as a visiting Professor at M.I.T. (Massachusetts Institute of Technology). Later we went out for a meal with them at Gadsby's near the hotel.

We travelled from Boston to Wilmington, in Delaware, the first State of America and the longest journey of our holiday, 300 miles. On the way to Wilmington we came through Rhode Island which is known as the "Ocean State", and incidentally, is the smallest State. We also came through New York and New Jersey, known as the "Garden State". Upon arriving in Wilmington, Delaware, we checked in at the Sheraton Brandy Wine Hotel in the Brandy Wine district where a fierce battle took place during the American Revolution. George Washington led his troops to fight against the British Army and it was the only battle of the American Revolution that the British Army won. Next door to the hotel we went into the enormous Concorde Shopping Mall, where there were good facilities for wheelchairs. In one part of the Mall we saw exhibits of Corvette Sports Cars, some new, some older.

One evening we drove into downtown Wilmington to Constantino's restaurant for a super succulent prime rib of beef: it was one and a half inches thick and weighed over 1lb. An absolutely fantastic meal! The following day we visited Washington D.C., the capital of the United States of America. We drove through the State capital of Maryland Baltimore en route to Washington. Upon arriving in Washington we saw the State capitol building on Capitol Hill, the White House at 1600 Pennsylvania Avenue, the Lincoln Memorial, the Needle (Washington Monument) and the New Vietnam War Memorial which was a life-size bronze sculpture of two army officers, one white and one coloured, and a long marble memorial inscribed in honour of the men who fell in battle. It was a very moving experience. There were a few kerbs around the place and an odd ramp here and there, and bumpy roads to cross.

Later we drove over the Potomac River into Virginia and saw Arlington Cemetery where J.F. Kennedy's grave is and where his eternal flame burns – and also the famous Pentagon building.

The following day we travelled from Wilmington to Bethany Beach on the Delaware coast to visit our friends the Perrinos for a few days. We stayed in their super rented apartment where they stayed each year. The interior had a lot of attractive wooden panelling with paintings of seagulls and boats on the walls. We visited a large marina called Indian River Inlet and went along the jetty to see all the huge fishing boats which cost between $500,000-$1,000,000 and above. The fishing boats go out for distances up to 60 miles catching blue fish, macho shark, blue marlins, etc. There was also a great showcase showing various models of fish, including the blue marlin, with its sword-like protrusion from the mouth. We collected a macho shark from a friend of Al Perrino's which was caught the day before. Then we drove on to a fish shop where we bought clams, live lobsters, blue fish and mussels before heading back to the apartment to prepare a meal. I held a live lobster on my lap with precautionary bands on its claws. The evening meal we prepared with our friends at Bethany Beach was absolutely fantastic. To start with we had a clam chowder, a type of soup, followed by mussels, blue fish, macho shark and finally lobster. It was one of the best fish meals I had ever had.

The following day we went onto the beautiful sandy beach, which stretched a long way. While the others swam and did some "Bogie Boarding," I sat on a wooden platform chatting to Al's wife, Betty and generally taking in the activities. Later we visited the Indian River Inlet Marina to see all the fishing boats coming in with their catch. This particular day was a poor fish-

64

ing day, and no blue fish were caught. We went to see a horse-shoe crab, an ugly-looking creature – we could not see a live one but picked up a dead one. This crab is the oldest living creature in the world, dating back to prehistoric times.

We all went down the coast in Al's huge limo, a Lincoln (in which I had my first experience of electrically operated car seats). The first stop-off was Bethany, a pretty town with a few shops, with a nicely-carved Indian totem pole. Next stop-off was to see a new housing development. The houses were absolutely beautiful, built on stilts to protect them from severe weather storms. We saw a plot of land which Al had bought – he was awaiting new housing laws to be passed by the Reagan administration. The houses on the development cost upwards of $500,000.

We then continued travelling on to Ocean City, in Maryland, at the end of the peninsula, a holiday resort and conference centre. A rapidly growing town, it is quite built up with lots of hotels and holiday apartments. We saw the old part of the town which was attractive. We drove near The Boardwalk, a wooden promenade, quite famous in America. On our return we picked up some seafood for the evening meal. It was another delicious meal comprising clams, mussels, crabs and spaghetti. It was a great experience breaking up the crabs with our fingers and small hammers, what a mess! We left the apartment the same night and travelled back to Wilmington, arriving at our hotel just after 1am.

The following day, our last day in America, we travelled back to New York's J.F.K. airport via Philadelphia. In Philadelphia we passed the J.F.K Stadium, venue for a forthcoming Live Aid Concert in aid of Ethiopian famine relief. We walked around the Independence Hall, Congress Hall and the old City Hall with the famous Liberty Bell close by enclosed in a glass structure. We spent some time in the shopping Galleria nearby called "The Bourse" the site of the former Stock

Exchange. We had a light meal there before continuing on our journey to New York. We came through Princeton, New Jersey, a famous Ivy League university town, then on to the New Jersey Turn Pike (toll road). We drove over the George Washington Bridge into New York then through the Bronx onto the J.F.K. Hilton at the airport. Once there we saw Concorde taxi-ing from the bedroom window

The following day Dad and I flew back on Concorde, leaving Mum and my sister Christine to fly back subsonic on a 747 . We flew on one of the new livery Concordes, G-BOAF. There was a Jetway to the plane door which made it easier, and Dad and I sat in the front row of the plane. Inside the new livery Concorde the seats are space age grey leather. The carpets also are space age grey with a red stripe running through them.

My wheelchair went into a cupboard. There were computer displays in front of us which tell you how many miles on the journey (New York J.F.K. to London Heathrow is 3,600 miles), the temperature outside (which dropped to -58° Centigrade), the Mach numbers which indicate the aircraft's speed (Mach One speed is around 650 miles per hour) and the altitude (Concordes cruise up to ten miles high).

We flew out of J.F.K. on the South East runway at 11.42am American time, waited for the flying Tigers freight aircraft to take off and then waited a few more seconds so we didn't catch up with the plane in front of us. When the pilot let the brake off the plane was off like a bullet, roaring like a tornado. It took us approximately five seconds to reach 100 mph; twenty minutes later the plane reached Mach One then the pilot put the boosters on, which felt like a slight nudge in the back, and off we went to reach Mach Two, twice the speed of sound. We were at Mach Two for two and a half hours, because the American Air Force were not using the flight path taken by Concorde as it was American Independence day, July 4th.

Concorde stretches eight inches in flight, due to the friction.

The sky is darker because of the height reached. When you reach Mach One the windows became warm, also due to friction. On a clear day you can see the curvature of the earth. I went into the cockpit which was fantastic: there is a very sophisticated network of controls, switches etc. Concorde has a special system called 'reheat' which injects fuel into the turbines. The nose of the plane can drop down hydraulically to 12 degrees maximum when landing for greater visibility and also drops slightly when taking off. We had a manual landing and touched down at 7.55pm English time, after a flight of three hours 13 minutes. The flight, take-off and landing were absolutely sensational, fantastic, brilliant, fabulous, remarkable! We were met off the plane by an airport official. There was a wait for Mum and my sister's plane to arrive from New York, before we all set off to drive back home to Chester.

Chapter 12

Fourth Trip to America, July 1986

Midwest, Illinois, Missouri, Kansas, Orlando, Florida

When I was 19, in July 1986, we flew from Manchester to Chicago on our fourth trip to the United States of America, on an American Airlines Boeing 767 with a flight time of eight hours 15 minutes.

As usual it was important that my wheelchair went into the hold of the plane and out at our destination. An airport official pushed me to the Jetway in the airport. Dad had to lift me 30 rows up the plane. We flew to Chicago O'Hare Airport. Our hotel in Chicago overlooked the Chicago River and Lake Michigan which is like a sea. We watched a number of speedboats and cruisers going up the Chicago River from our hotel window.

The following day, after a leisurely breakfast, we went up Chicago's Sears Tower which was the tallest building in the world – it is 110 storeys high. We went up to the sky deck level of the tower on the 103rd floor, 1,353ft high, and had a fantastic vista of Chicago, seeing such things as the boat marinas on Michigan's shore, Chicago River, the beautiful Buckingham Fountain, and huge rail yards and tracks. The overall height of the Sears Tower is 1,707ft. Inside the tower there was a ramp to the lift area.

Chicago – the Windy City – is regarded as America's architectural

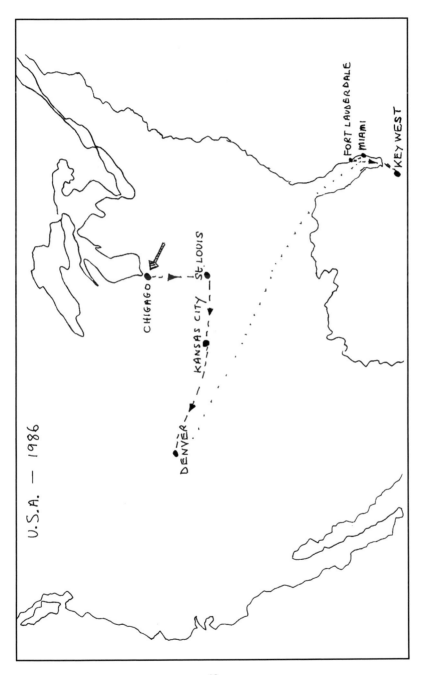

masterpiece, it is also one of the world's major trade and transportation centres. It was extremely hot: 70% humidity in 100 degree Fahrenheit temperatures and the heat generated from the cars made it even worse, so we went into a shopping mall called The Watertower to cool off! It was quite a shock to the system to go from the intense heat outside to the air conditioned environment inside.

We strolled to Oak Street beach on Lake Michigan's shore which was absolutely teeming with people. There were a lot of people water ski-ing and sailing. I went down a ramped subway to the beach and heard the sound of a saxophonist echoing some lovely music which added to the atmosphere.

There was quite a number of steep kerbs to negotiate, but there were ramps in some places. The pavements were comparatively flat apart from odd cracks about the place but the terrain presented no serious difficulties.

In the evening we went to a restaurant in Chicago called Shuckers. A 'shucker' is a person who opens clams, oysters and mussels. In the restaurant there was a flight of stairs not much wider than my chair; Dad negotiated most of the stairs then my headrest fell off as he slipped back slightly on the bend. My chair was resting on the stairs but somehow or other we managed. Going down the stairs my Dad lifted the chair down first and then carried me down.

Chicago is a very clean city with lots of things to see and do. It is surprising what we managed to see in a day. The following morning, before leaving, we drove along the shores of Lake Michigan for a short distance looking at a fabulous marina with many fairly large yachts and pleasure cruisers.

The next destination of our hols was St. Louis in the state of Missouri, a distance of 300 miles. We travelled through a lot of farmland with field upon field of alfalfa, a crop grown for fodder. We went past a number of ranches and stopped at Springfield, the State capital of Illinois, which is the birthplace of Abraham Lincoln. He lived in the city from 1844 to 1861, where he raised a family, practised law and died there. We saw Abraham Lincoln's house preserved as a national monument. We walked into the visitors' centre nearby which was wheelchair-friendly!

As we left Springfield we passed the elegant state capitol building, with its lovely rotunda dome. Outside the main town there were a lot of beautiful houses – the majority constructed from wood. Springfield also possessed a lot of parkland, at least, that was my impression. We proceeded to drive to St. Louis and as we got closer could see the Gateway Arch shining in the distance, a huge structure. Our hotel room in St. Louis overlooked the Arch and the Mississippi River. The Arch, which dominates the St. Louis skyline, is 680 feet long and represents the Gateway to the West. It was designed by Eero Saarinen and constructed in 1965 from stainless steel.

The following day we visited the Museum of Westward Expansion located underneath the Gateway Arch. There was a ramp into the museum. In there we saw how much Man has progressed, achieved and discovered over the last 100 years. We also saw what facilities and equipment men and women had during this time on their journeys westward. We saw many exhibits such as a stagecoach, a stuffed grizzly bear and a stuffed appaloosa horse (Indian pony). It was a very interesting museum. We walked along the waterfront by the muddy fast flowing Mississippi river, which is 2,348 miles long. There was a ramp down to the waterfront which helped a lot. We saw a few paddle steamers including one called *President*. We walked around Lacledes landing, named after a New Orleans fur trader called Pierre Lacledes, which is the only remaining part of the original city of St. Louis. There were a lot of old cannery buildings which are now offices, shops, cafés and restaurants. The city had nice cobblestone streets in parts, though they were not much good for wheelchairs. Some were very bumpy with steep inclines for Dad in the intense heat – but there was no problem, he was strong enough to manoeuvre the chair. Later, we walked into the St. Louis Centre, an enormous shopping Galleria. It was a very modern white building with lots of water features. The shops, cafés and restaurants were very nice and cool. As I've mentioned before, it is quite a shock to the body going from the heat outside into to cool, air conditioned temperatures in the shops and hotels. Across the road from our hotel was the Busch Memorial Stadium, the home of the St. Louis baseball team the Cardinals, who were playing on the day we were there. We decided to walk over to the stadium during the game and were able to peep through a gap to glimpse what was going on. When the team scored the cheers from the crowds were very loud and mixed in with banging noises, which contributed to a fantastic, electric atmosphere. It certainly got the adrenalin going – a good ending to the day!

The following day's destination was Kansas City 350 miles away. Incidentally, Kansas City, Kansas is next door to Kansas City in the state of Missouri! On the journey we travelled through lush greenery and field upon field of corn and a number of small towns. We stayed in a Kansas City, Kansas hotel for a couple of nights. Later on we drove into downtown Kansas, Missouri to find a restaurant called the Golden Ox for our evening meal. It was located in an old cattle stockyard which was once part of the many cattle holding yards around. The Golden Ox is famous for a big succulent steak known as the 'Kansas City Strip', which we all ate.

The following day we visited the Plaza area of Kansas City, Missouri. The Plaza was a particularly beautiful area with fountains and statues and many shops, some exclusive, such as Gucci. The architecture was Spanish, modelled after buildings in Seville.

Next stop off was Westport, an old area of Kansas City, Missouri where the buildings were mainly red brick dating back to 1840. An old trolley bus passed by as we were walking around the area. Later we visited the Westin Crown Centre Hotel complex – a massive place with numerous shops. In the hotel foyer area there were some cascading waterfalls 60 feet high. We bought our tea here from a Deli Bar – massive sandwiches doused with delightful relishes and meats, such as pastrami.

We drove from Kansas City, Kansas to Denver, Colorado at 600 miles the longest single journey of the holiday. En route we travelled through lush green countryside in East Kansas and saw quite a number of cattle grazing. We passed Topeka, the State capital of Kansas where there are numerous oil wells. Then we travelled through field upon field of wheat for about 200 miles and saw many huge grain silos all over the land. There were four massive silos joined together that stood by a railway to facilitate the transport of the grain to the farms and markets in other parts of the U.S.A.

We stayed in Denver for a few nights. The elevation of Denver is 5,286ft above sea level, at the very foot of the Rocky Mountains, so it is aptly named the 'Mile High City'. It was founded in 1858 by gold-seekers. While we were in Denver we saw the skyscrapers which you see in the television soap opera *Dynasty*. I think Denver is a well-laid out, very clean and sophisticated city. It was there we saw the Colorado State capitol building.

I thought the altitude of this 'Mile High City' would make breathing difficult but this was no problem to me. The pavements were flat, with plenty of ramps about the place, although there was the odd kerb to negotiate. Outside the downtown area we saw lots of parkland and beautiful homesteads. One day we drove from Denver to Colorado Springs, travelling through lots of hilly land with unusual rock formations. Pikes Peak, at 14,110ft, is the highest mountain in the Colorado Springs area with excellent views of the countryside.

In one area there were lots of red sandstone boulders on the roadside with trees growing out of them. After Colorado Springs we drove through Manitou Springs, seeing many log cabins on the mountain sides. Then we travelled round the back of Pikes Peak seeing all the fantastic and awe-inspiring scenery. There were numerous fir trees on the mountains around us with still quite a lot of snow carpeting the mountain summits. The Rockies looked spectacular as we drove through Cripple Creek, a Western town, and saw many old gold-mine buildings and chutes in which the ore used to come down in the heyday of the gold rush. There are still some gold-mining activities being carried out in the area, assisted by more modern technology. From Cripple Creek we drove on a narrow red shale track called Phantom Canyon Road, an apt name for this road, with its 27 miles of very bumpy track with many cracks in it. It was a scenic route with huge boulders on the mountainsides and many trees growing out of them. We travelled through a few tunnels with just room enough for one car. A stream threaded its way through part of the area. The track we were on was built to carry freight, gold and passengers to the main towns in this area in the 1820s. At the next stop-off we visited the Royal Gorge and drove over a suspension bridge 1,053ft above the Arkansas River which runs through this gorgeous gorge. It is the highest suspension bridge in the world. Nearby we saw some deer feeding on the roadside.

The following day we journeyed to Estes Park via the town of Boulder where we stopped for another good old American breakfast. We saw many boulders, more with trees growing out of them, and many fast running streams with water cascades. The snow-crowned Rockies looked spectacular. We arrived in the beautiful Estes Park, high mountain valley, in the late morning and walked around part of it. There were a few kerbs to negotiate with an odd ramp. We saw Lake Estes, complete with windsurfer. Towering above the lake was Mount

Above left: King Charles spaniel;
above right: golden retriever;
below left: airedale;
below right: owl (on stone).

Right: My favourite, a European eagle owl painted on slate, which I could have sold many times.

Below: mice painted on stone.

d

Olympus. There are lots of log cabins in and around Estes Park.

As we travelled into the Rocky Mountain National Park, to Bear Lake, we saw lush green pastures, and a few glaciers and snowfields on the mountain slopes. Bear Lake was crystal clear, with beautiful pine trees surrounding it and spectacular mountains.

A bird I spotted in this area was called a Stellers Jay. It had a black head and a beautiful dark blue plumage. It was bumpy pushing the chair near to the lake but we encountered no great difficulty. At one point Dad splashed some water from the lake onto my face – it was nice and cool and refreshing.

From Denver we flew to Miami, Florida. During the flight whilst Dad went to the loo, there was a spell of nasty turbulence and I felt as though I was going to fall forwards, so I nudged the man next to me from his slumber and asked him to put his hand in front of me to prevent this from happening. With steel rods in my spine it is important that I am not bent or jerked suddenly too far forward, which causes unnecessary stress on my spine and on me! An unexpected bonus during our flight was that we had to circle around in a holding position before landing. During this time we had excellent views, for about an hour, of the expansive Everglades eco-system and Miami Beach.

In Florida we stayed in Fort Lauderdale, the 'Venice of America', 30 miles east of Miami. Our hotel was by the beach and I swam in the Atlantic Ocean which was warm with crystal clear bluey green water. Dad had to lift me and carry me 100 yards into the sea. I got dressed after my swim on a sun bed – it was a bit of a struggle and I found it uncomfortable on the wooden slats, but we managed.

One night we had dinner at Shirttail Charlie's by the inland waterways. I had alligator to eat which was quite an experience! It took a bit of chewing, though. I was wild after it! Later we drove down Las Olas Boulevard, it was a particularly beautiful area with lots of nice shops on either side of the road, lined with palm trees and we saw lots of fabulous homes, apartments and superb boats lit up. It was a lovely sight to see.

Another day we went on the Jungle Queen boat cruise. There was a ramp to get on board. The trip took three hours during which we observed lots of beautiful houses and fantastic boats. The houses cost between about $400,000 - $2,500,000, while some of the boats there cost between $6,000,000 - $12,000,000. We stopped off at Jungle Queen Island on which Florida's Seminole Indians live. They have never signed a treaty with the United States of America.

We saw one of the Indians wrestling alligators. He hypnotised one of them and called it over to him, then he held the alligator's mouth wide open, stroked it, shook one of its webbed feet and then flicked his fingers to wake it up. Alligators can weigh up to one ton and they have 88 teeth. It was quite a 'different' experience watching the alligator wrestling. On the journey back to the marina I spotted a brightly coloured iguana walking across a garden. We saw the H.M.S. *Ark Royal* docked in Lauderdale and an ocean-going liner called the *Cleopatra* which was recently used in the T.V. series *Miami Vice*.

The following day we travelled down the Florida Keys which are 160 miles long. The Keys are islands and islets largely composed of coral and limestone that are linked together by causeways. The first was called Key Largo. There was also a bridge seven miles long. The bluey green and purplish sea was on either side of the road. We saw many ospreys' nests, which at the time I thought were storks' nests, perched atop of telegraph poles. There were many marinas on the Keys with some fabulous fishing vessels and many lovely apartments with palm trees everywhere – it was like paradise. We observed many pelicans by the marinas. In some areas we saw mangrove swamps. At the end of the Keys we stopped off at Key

West, a nice town with lots of old colonial-style buildings with beautiful private beaches. I had a coffee and Key lime pie in Sloppy Joe's. It's a famous Floridorian pudding like a lemon meringue pie but made with limes.

We drove to the southernmost point of continental America at Key West, which is 90 miles from Cuba, and arrived back in Fort Lauderdale later that night.

On the last day we drove along the coast from Fort Lauderdale as far as Palm Beach, and saw many absolutely beautiful houses, apartments and hotels with fabulous well manicured gardens and lots of private beaches. We travelled back to Miami ready to fly home and I was taken down to the aircraft by an official. It was quite a distance – I travelled by monorail part of the way and then there was some more walking until we reached the satellite, a circular building with Jetways radiating off to the various aircraft including our 747. Dad carried me 39 rows into the plane for our journey home. Shortly after take-off we experienced an electrical storm which added a bit of colour to an otherwise pitch black sky. It soon passed.

When the plane arrived in London we were met by a British Airways official and taken through the new Terminal 4 building with its ramps all over the place, lifts and good facilities for the disabled. The B.A. official arranged for a bus with a lift on the back to take us to Terminal 1. We had to drive fairly quickly to Terminal 1 to get the plane shuttle up to Manchester. The chair went into the hold of the plane, and came out at Manchester. We were met off the plane at Manchester. Everything went very smoothly which was brilliant. An excellent holiday!

Chapter 12

Fifth Trip to America, October 1987

California

I was now 20 years old, and this holiday was the first in which I played a major part, planning the itinerary and reading information and a bit of historical fact. We had been to California before on a previous trip so it was planned to visit new places we had not seen before such as Yosemite National Park, which had been closed on the first visit because of excessive snow falls. Lake Tahoe was also somewhere we planned to go and Mendocino was chosen for its interesting coastline. It was also good to re-visit places we'd enjoyed the previous time.

On this particular holiday we flew to San Francisco, a flying time of nine hours 45 minutes. Upon arriving at San Francisco International Airport, after going through the usual formalities, we picked up a Chevrolet Celebrity hire car and headed for Berkeley, which is across the bay of San Francisco over the Oakland Bay Bridge. We stayed at the Berkerley Marriott Hotel where we had a 'disabled room' which gave us more space and made things easier. At the back of the hotel is the Berkerley Marina where there were lots of fantastic boats, yachts and cruisers. You can go on trips around the San Francisco Bay from the marina.

The following day after a leisurely breakfast overlooking the marina we travelled into downtown San Francisco. We parked by the Fisherman's Wharf which was near to the Travel Lodge where we stayed during our first visit to the USA in April 1979. We passed the *Balclutha* boat which is a fully rigged sailing ship of the Cape Horn fleet. Incidentally, Alcatraz Island lies 2.4 km. off Fisherman's Wharf. Its most infamous prisoner was Al Capone, who when registering, wrote defiantly, as his occupation, "gangster." We spent some time looking around Fisherman's Wharf, observing fresh fish such as crabs, lobsters and clams – there was a lovely smell of fish! Our next stop-off on this walking tour was the Golden Gate recreational area, where there is a small beach. At one point Dad said, "Look at that great big rusty propeller," to which my reply was, "Where?" Dad retorted, "There, directly in front of you!" We saw the Golden Gate Bridge looming through the mist emanating from the Pacific Ocean. We proceeded on to Ghirardelli Square through Victorian Park, a slight incline to negotiate, but we had no problem because Dad was strong and able to push the wheelchair. Ghirardelli Square is a huge shopping and dining complex which has been created from an old chocolate factory. Near the entrance was an attractive fountain which gave a nice cooling effect. The next destination was Washington Square to view Coit Tower on Telegraph Hill which was fashioned on a fire hose nozzle as a tribute to the City's fire fighters by Lillie Hitchcock Coit.

We stopped off for a light lunch at Calzones, an Italian restaurant – I had a huge shrimp with ham wrapped around it on a bed of salad topped with a spicy dressing. The restaurant was decked out by numerous shelves on which were displayed a vast array of tinned foodstuffs, such as tomatoes, sauces, fish and meats. There were also sausages and onions hanging down from the shelves. Food for thought and everywhere!

After we lunch strolled into Chinatown, which has the largest population of Chinese citizens outside China. Chinese music was echoing down the street adding to the atmosphere. We looked at numerous shops selling interesting Chinese

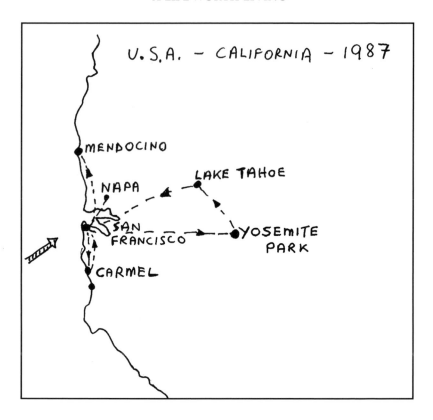

U.S.A. - CALIFORNIA - 1987

MENDOCINO

NAPA

LAKE TAHOE

SAN FRANCISCO

YOSEMITE PARK

CARMEL

wares, including many food places selling live fish etc. Later, we drove again down the famous crooked Lombard Street. We had driven down it eight years before in 1979.

San Francisco is not an ideal place for negotiating a wheel-chair although it is not too bad in parts. We noticed how much the city had been built up since our first trip there in 1979. After sightseeing we travelled back to the hotel for a swim and a nice hot and refreshing Jacuzzi. That evening we had a meal at Trader Vic's, a Polynesian Continental Restaurant. The interior was Polynesian with face masks hanging on the walls and some type of longboat mounted from the ceiling. To start our meal we had *bongo-bongo* soup, which consisted of spinach, cream and oysters. The oysters together with the spinach are liquidised, then cream is poured over the whole surface of the soup and slightly browned. The next course I had was fresh salmon with a cheese sauce and 'caviar' - not the real stuff, it was coloured red and taken from the roe of a lumpfish.

The following day we visited Mendocino 120 miles north of San Francisco, crossing over the Richmond – San Rafael Bridge and immediately afterwards we saw the famous San Quentin Prison. We went through San Rafael, which is the administrative and commercial hub of Marin County, and travelled up the Sonoma Valley, a wine-growing area known as the 'Valley of the Moon'. The scenery was beautiful, the hillsides were lush green and lower down were the browns of parched grass. We had rain during this day, the first rain for nine months. At Cloverdale we drove on Highway 128 which crosses the Anderson Valley – the road became very steep and winding and the scenery reflected the full variety of autumn colours. We passed a restaurant called the New Booneville Restaurant which a friend had told us to look out for the day before, it was apparently California's finest, and had a fantastic herb and vegetable garden but sadly had to close a year after opening. The 'Moonies' religious sect started in Booneville about 12 years ago.

We observed the fantastic redwoods in a 15-mile tract of forest called Mallard Redwoods, 115 miles north of San Francisco. You could drive a car through some of these trees because of their massive girth. We saw the Navarro River in Mendocino County as we drove up Highway 1. Once again, I thought the coastline was comparable to Cornwall in its rugged beauty and steep winding roads. We stopped off at the Little River Inn, which is a white Maine-style building, an attractive wooden edifice dating back to 1858. We were planning to have a meal there but it was a Rotary Day and they were too busy. The town of Mendocino is quaint with a few shops and a beautiful white Presbyterian Church.

We had lunch at the Seagull Restaurant where I had red snapper ciappino in a casserole and a side salad served with Roquefort cheese dressing – delicious! We spent a couple of hours in Mendocino but it was pouring with rain so I was unable to look around the shops. There were high kerbs to negotiate the pavements but Mum looked around a few shops. It was here we bought a pot of boysenberry jam from the famous Marylyn Douglas Jam and Jellies shop which are sold all over the US.

There were whale lookout towers in Mendocino. You can see grey whales jumping here at this time approximately 400ft. from the shore. They migrate in the late summer from their feeding ground in the Bering Sea to Baja California coast in Mexico where they breed. It can be a 6,000 mile trip. Approximately 15,000 grey whales make the trip each year, the first whale arriving in Southern California in late December. On their return they are accompanied by their calves – and at the end of their journey they are famished.

On our way back to Berkeley we stopped off at the Heritage Inn which was used in the film, *Same Time Next Year* starring Allan Alder, of *M*A*S*H* fame, the popular TV comedy series based in a U.S. army hospital during the Korean War. We travelled back most of the same way as driving to Mendocino but diverted through more of Marin County which is very hilly with lots of houses perched on the hillsides and hilltops. There was quite a number of ranches with beautiful horses. We drove over the Golden Gate Bridge, and paid a toll of one dollar. We saw the San Francisco skyline, all lit up, from the bridge and then proceeded through downtown San Francisco. The evening lights in the town added a magical effect. We arrived back at the Marriott at 8pm and slept very well that night.

The following day we travelled to Yosemite Valley, driving through Oakland, a hilly lush green county. Then we came through the San Joaquin Valley, in which all the fruits you can think of are grown in its beautiful orchards. We drove over the 500-mile long San Joaquin aqueduct which carries the run-off from the Northern Californian Mountains to Los Angeles. On Highway 99 we could see the High Sierras in the distance getting closer and closer. The land was becoming more hilly with rocks scattered about the hillsides and hilltops with quite a number of trees. We began climbing higher and higher, seeing all the beautiful fir trees and lovely mountains. From Highway 99 we went onto Highway 140 at Merced, which is known as the Gateway to Yosemite and crosses the Silver Merced River, a V-shaped river-cut canyon.

As we entered Yosemite National Park the first rocky out crop we saw was Elportal and a short time later Bridal Veil Falls came into view, plunging 620 feet into the river below. It was a beautiful waterfall cascading like a flowing bridal train. We saw El Capitan towering 7,500ft above sea level which looked wonderful in the afternoon sunlight – it is often quoted as having the highest vertical wall on earth. A short time later Half Dome Mountain came into view, a famous Yosemite peak. which is over 9,000ft high. The scenery around was absolutely splendid, out of this world, with beautiful sequoia fir trees. I think Yosemite is like a cathedral without a roof and the high mountains like church organs playing resplendent music. The whole area was awe-inspiring. We stayed in Yosemite Lodge in a wooden cabin, a well-appointed 'disabled room' with ramps and a large bathroom area, which helped to make things easier. There were lots of deer around the cabin chewing away at the grass and one came up to it for a closer inspection. That evening we had dinner at the Ahwahnee Hotel which was a Swiss style building. The restaurant had a big banqueting hall and was two storeys high with very large rock pillars and massive windows which offered wonderful views of the alpine landscape, a fitting way to end the day.

The following day we woke early. It was great to watch the

My drawing of El Capitan

sunrise on Yosemite mountains – they looked beautiful bathed in soft golden sunlight. It was a frosty and crisp October morning. We enjoyed a really nice breakfast at the Four Seasons Restaurant before setting off to drive to Glacier Point, travelling over the 'Badger Pass' winter ski resort. There were innumerable beautiful trees: Douglas fir, sequoias, ponderosa and incense cedars. As we were driving, strands of ground mist were enveloping the car, creating a special atmosphere.

Glacier Point marks where the progress of the glacier was halted at the close of the ice age. At an elevation of 7,214ft it gives you a panoramic vista of Yosemite Valley, an awesome scene of beauty. The Half Dome peak looked majestic in the morning sunshine.

There was a long pathway, specially built for the disabled, which led to the observation point. It is said that "If God created the Universe he put his signature on Yosemite", which He did! We spent some time just beholding the sheer grandeur and magnificence of this cathedral-like sanctuary. From Glacier Point we travelled back into Yosemite Valley below, via the Badger Pass and into the rest of Yosemite National Park onto the Tioga road which led us to Lee Vining, which is just outside Yosemite. We planned to stay here for one night.

As we traversed this road the scenery revealed stark contrasts ranging from the rugged moraine (glacial debris) to alpine meadows. It is amazing to see how trees grow out of the rocks. Two inches of snow had fallen on this road two days before. We stopped off at Tenaya Lake in the Tenaya Canyon, named after an Indian chief of that name and saw a lot of glacial polish which made the rocks gleam like silver in the afternoon sunshine and more glacial debris strewn about the place. Another feature of glacial geographic sculpturing was huge inclined pavements of granite. These pavements were covered with many cracks creating a patchwork mosaic of rocks. We parked the car at the edge of Tenaya Lake where Mum got a cup of water from the lake and splashed it on my face, which was most refreshing. We travelled on through Tuolumne Meadows, massive alpine meadows with lovely carpets of trees.

We left Yosemite at the Tioga Pass entrance, elevation 9,141ft. It started to snow for a short time as we entered into Inyo National Forest. The Tioga pass was extremely steep and winding as we made the descent. We saw many trees in the distance with wonderful autumn tints en route to Lee Vining, which stands on the shore of Mono Lake. The lake is seven million years old and is one of America's oldest. It's more salty than ocean water and so gives greater buoyancy for swimming. "Mono" is the Yukots Indian name for brine fly.

Our hotel had a 'disabled room' which was very spacious and had a good bathroom.

The following day we visited Mono County State Park, where there was a avenue of trees at the entrance in beautiful bright yellows, oranges and ruby reds. It was here we saw unusual rock formations called Tufa Towers (pronounced Toofah) which looked as though they belonged to another planet in the solar system, or the Moon!

From Lee Vining we drove to Lake Tahoe and on the way visited a real ghost town called Bodie, after William S. Bodie who found gold here in 1859. In 1879 the town boasted a population of 10,000. I could not get out of the vehicle here because the terrain was too rough for my wheelchair, with glass splinters and nails scattered about. So I saw this part of the town from the car park. A short time after leaving on the 13 miles of rocky track, we spotted a huge grey owl perched on a post; it wasn't until later that I realised it was, in fact, the Great Grey Owl. Some miles later we passed some fabulous large ranches with beautiful horses in the paddocks. It was here I saw a number of birds of prey, probably falcons and buzzards, perched on the fences. We stopped off for brunch where I had "Pigs in a

Blanket" - a large sausage wrapped in a pancake. We then pro-
ceeded to Lake Tahoe whose water was the colour of Quink
Ink. It was flanked by the High Sierra Mountains. We passed
Emerald Bay, a truly beautiful three-mile long appendage to
Lake Tahoe. We had a fantastic view of the bay and Fanetta
Island from the highway, a few hundred feet above the lake
surface.

We then drove onto the Sunnyside Hotel at Lake Tahoe, near
Tahoe City, where we had a beautiful apartment-like 'disabled
room' with lovely pine furniture. The room had plenty of space
with a perfect vista of the lake.

We drove around the lake the next day and passed the
Squaw Valley Ski Resort which hosted the Winter Olympics of
1960. Next we stopped off at a place called Donner, where a
contingent of 89 people called the Donner Party came from
Springfield Illinois led by Captain Donner in 1846. They were
attempting to reach the Pacific coast to try and start a new life.
When the party arrived here they were snowed in by a fall of
22ft of snow; 47 of them died of starvation and exposure.

We continued driving around the Tahoe shoreline which is
71 miles long, parting California from the state of Nevada.
Lake Tahoe is also the eighth deepest lake in the world.

There are lots of gambling halls and casinos around the lake
particularly on the Nevada side. We did some gambling at
Harrah's on the slot machine, and won about 20 dollars – it
was exciting watching the cents cascading out of the machine.
Our winnings bought our lunch! We had the most delicious
fish and chips, the best I have ever tasted. The fish was sea
bass. Later we watched the sunset over Emerald Bay, with fabulous streaks of pink, red and purple tinges.

The following day we journeyed to the Napa Valley, the
world-famous wine-producing region. The first winery we visited was the Robert Mondavi vineyard, it was here we saw the
massive traditional oak wine vats and the modern metal ones.

There were huge heaters outside to keep the vines at the correct temperature. The next vineyard was the Beaulieu winery and in an attractive wooden panelled room that I thought resembled the interior of a modern church we sampled some wines: 1986 Sauvignon Blanc, 1985 Pinot Chardonnay, 1985 Pinot Noir and 1984 Cabernet Sauvignon. The wines were up to scratch and went down like a Cadillac. In the nearby town of St. Helena we saw the house used in the soap opera, *Falcon Crest*, which is part of the Spring Mountain winery. We viewed the house through the trees from a distance.

Napa Valley is a beautiful area with lush rolling hills and has over 160 wineries. Another vineyard we visited was the Preger Winery and Port Works. I stayed in the car, since it was raining, and watched the owner and his son picking grapes. Mr Preger had only been in the wine industry for five years – he was previously an insurance broker and he worked a small plot of one acre. He was also interested in the production of port.

We stayed in a beautiful hotel called the Vintage Inn. Our room was like an apartment with lovely hand-printed designs on the drapery. There were nice wooden shutters, a fireplace where we lit a fire and a Jacuzzi. There was plenty of room to manoeuvre the wheelchair. In the grounds, close to the room was a channel filled with water and fountains called the Alhambran Waterway, apparently built to drown out the noise of traffic. That evening we had a meal in the hotel restaurant; I had swordfish with mange tout, rice and red and yellow peppers. We washed the meal down with Robert Pepi white wine.

The next day we drove on to Carmel and on the way we went to the San Juan Bautista Mission – the largest of the Father Junipero Sierras Missions which was founded in 1797. Its chapel had Spanish and Mexican decorations. The other attractions at the mission site included stables, a carriage house, attractive gardens and orchards. The San Andreas Fault lies in the valley which runs very close to the church.

We continued on the journey to Carmel via Monterey where we saw field upon field of artichokes – Monterey is the artichoke capital of the world. There are also many golf courses in the Carmel and Monterey area. We stayed at a very pleasant Spanish-style mansion with the most beautiful gardens. Outside our room we had a wonderfully fragrant Angel Trumpet Tree.

The following morning at 7.00am we strolled from our hotel to Carmel Beach which had lovely white sand and fabulous Monterey cypress trees. It was nice to hear the waves crashing on the beach – a tranquil time of the day.

Later we visited Monterey Aquarium which was converted from an old cannery building in 1984 and houses 5,000 native sea creatures. Outside the aquarium we saw a colony of shag seabirds and a group of seals on the rocks. It was a most interesting aquarium, and I particularly enjoyed watching the sea otters. They also had a huge, cathedral-like kelp forest exhibit. Kelp is a type of seaweed which grows up to 200ft high. We heard some interesting commentaries about the aquarium and its exhibits. As we walked down Cannery Row, there were many old cannery buildings to see which had been converted to shops and art galleries. The American author John Steinbeck immortalised the area in his book *Cannery Row*. We had coffee in a pleasant restaurant which had wooden panelling and was adorned with fishing nets and other maritime equipment.

From Monterey we drove on Highway 1 along the Pacific Coast where the scenery was quite spectacular, with sheer drops and hairpin bends. We stopped off for lunch at Nepenthe – *nepenthe,* from the Greek, means "without sorrow". Orson Welles built this place for his wife Rita Heyworth. It was 800ft above the azure Pacific Ocean. I had an ambrosia burger with kosher pickle, which was delicious! We sat outside soaking up the sunshine. Close by, we saw a phoenix carved out of a piece of redwood with copper legs. Later we drove back to Carmel and had a good walk around the quaint streets with their exquisite shops. As a matter of interest, Clint Eastwood the famous actor, was the Mayor of Carmel. Then we drove back to Carmel's beach and saw a wonderful sunset shining across the ocean, its rays radiating like searchlights into the sky.

The following day we travelled back to Berkeley for our last night and went out to dinner with some friends. The restaurant where we dined was built on stilts and we could see the skyline of San Francisco which looked magical all lit up. We had some different foods such as sushi (Japanese raw fish), raw squid and raw tuna. For the main course I had an Hawaiian fish called *maihe-maihe*, followed by a delicious whisky cake. It was a very pleasant evening.

We spent our last morning in downtown San Francisco walking around Macy's, the famous American store. We had a coffee at the Hyatt Hotel and enjoyed a fantastic panoramic view of the bay dotted with yachts. Then we made our way to the airport for our flight home to Heathrow via Vancouver.

Chapter 14

Christianity:
Becoming close to the Lord

In mid-November 1986, when I was 19, Mum and I read a book written by an American lady called Joni Eareckson. It was her third book and was called *Choices and Changes*. Nineteen years previously, when she was 17, she had broken her neck in a diving accident, leaving her paralysed in four limbs – a quadriplegic. Then I read her first book, *Joni,* and another book entitled *A Step Further*. Her courage, finding a new meaning in life and her faith in God, is amazing. She has spoken to people all over America and in other parts of the world about her faith. People worldwide write to her for guidance, advice and encouragement so in 1979 she started a ministry called Joni and Friends. There is a movie named *Joni* and also a short film called *Reflections of His Love*. After reading her books and watching the film, she inspired me enormously and I felt myself becoming closer to the Lord. I accepted Jesus in a new way as my Lord and Saviour from sin. Most days now I think of Jesus on the cross on the hill in Jerusalem and the resurrection and say to myself that he died for me and everybody because he loves us so much. God shows his love for us in that while we were still yet sinners Christ died for us. (*Romans 5 verse 8*).

I never realised how great God's love is, greater than anything in all creation. One of my favourite Bible verses which expresses God's love is: "I have loved you with an everlasting Love therefore I have drawn you with loving kindness." (*Jeremiah 33*).

I wrote a letter to Joni Eareckson for some advice on my autobiography and got a reply which was very helpful. I feel much happier in myself since becoming closer to the Lord. I was happy in myself before but it's given me more meaning in life. The local Revd. John Malbon comes fortnightly to give me Communion at home. He gets me videos on the Bible and insights about God which have been a great help. If we put our sins and anxieties at the foot of the cross after saying a prayer accepting the Lord as our Saviour into our lives, we will receive spiritual healing and this will start us on the incredible journey and adventure. God will refresh us on our journey, inspire and encourage us.

Once, I went to Chester and my hands got cold and the weight of my jacket made it very difficult to control my electric wheelchair. I could hardly move my chair and I kept saying to myself, "Every mountain can be climbed, every battle can be won, God is on the side that says, It can be done." When I got back to the van I thanked God for his strength. Here is a little verse I wrote at that time about God's power:

Oh how incredible God's Power and constant Love is,

That His Love will not let us go, no matter what happens to us in this

Lifetime he will never leave us,

Oh how incredible is his gift of healing to you and to me. And

If we believe in Him we shall not perish and we will have eternal life (*John 3 v 16*)

Oh how incredible God's providence is, Praise the Sovereign Lord.

Every morning I read a portion of the Bible. I learned that it is best to read the Scripture before approaching God in prayer because this provides the right climate and sets prayers off in the right direction. I read this in a small book called *Prayer Diary*, from the Crusade for Worldwide Revival. The book was very helpful. Also at this time I spent some time reading about the Psalms in the *Lion Handbook to the Bible*: the Psalms express the full range of human feelings from sadness to happiness, and from dark depression to exuberant joy. Psalm 42 verse 1 is a lovely verse, "As a deer longs for streams of living water so I long for you Lord." C. S. Lewis said, "Psalms are poems intended to be sung not doctrinal treatises or even sermons. They are to be read as Psalms if they are to be understood, otherwise we shall miss what is there and think we see what is not."

Since becoming closer to the Lord I pray much more. There is a nice piece of Scripture, "Pray in the Spirit on all occasions with all kinds of prayers and requests, with this in mind be alert and keep praying." (*Ephesians 6 verse 18*).

In 1987, a friend, the Revd. Peter Leakey, sent us a letter telling us that Joni Eareckson and her husband Ken were coming to the Free Trade Hall in Manchester on their tour of England. We managed to get tickets to see Joni on 25th June – the last night of the tour. The *Christian Herald* newspaper editor, Colin Reeves, started the evening off by introducing a Christian pop group from Australia called Chris Pringle – it was a good group, very loud, with lights flashing all over the stage.

Joni and her husband Ken came on stage to loud applause. She sang her tribute to God, "Joni's Waltz", which is lovely, then she proceeded to talk about how she met her husband. Joni also shared lots of spiritual insights and talked about her organisation, Joni and Friends. Some slides were projected on a very large screen to show aspects of her ministry, including her paintings done by mouth. There were about 18 other people in wheelchairs in the hall, where numbers were restricted by the fire regulations. Joni told us she was going on a tour of East Germany, Hungary and Czechoslovakia, visiting rehabilitation centres, hospitals and churches. Later we met the Revd.

Peter Leakey and his wife Diane who had come to see Joni along with members of their new church in Manchester.

Later in 1987, I met the Revd John Hayes at a service in Barrow Church and afterwards at a choir party. We talked about services in church and I expressed an interest in taking part in a service. Subsequently, he called to see me on several occasions. I got to know him better during 1989. In 1989 there was a Mission England rally run by the Billy Graham Mission Organisation. It was during this time that the Revd. Hayes asked me if I would like to do my testimony in Church and so arrangements were made to do my Christian Testimony on Sunday, 7th May.

Before the service I felt a little nervous, but as soon as I got up to talk I was very relaxed through God's powerful presence. The church was fairly full, and lots of the family and friends came to give me moral support. Below is what I had to say:

MY CHRISTIAN TESTIMONY

"In mid-November 1986, Mum and I read a book written by an American lady called Joni Eareckson called *Choices and Changes*, her third book. Twenty two years ago she broke her neck in a diving accident, leaving her paralysed in four limbs a quadriplegic. After reading her book she inspired me enormously and felt myself coming closer to God, I accepted Jesus in a new way, as My Lord and Saviour from Sin. I recommend that you read these books especially *Choices and Changes*. Most days now I think of Jesus on the cross and the resurrection and say to myself he died for me and everyone, because he loved us so much. God came out of the glory of heaven to earth to sympathise with our weakness (*Rom. 5 v 8*). God shows us his love for us in that while we were yet sinners Christ died for us. I never realised how great God's love was before, greater than anything in all creation. One of my favourite Bible verses which expresses God's love for us is *Jer. 33 v 1* - "I have loved you with an everlasting love, therefore I have drawn you with loving kindness." I feel much happier in myself since becoming closer to the Lord. I was happy in myself before but it has given me a lot more meaning in life and JOY. However, I must set my heart on things above where my heart belongs (*Col. 3 v 2*). I am setting my heart on things above, one thing I can look forward to is the day when I get my new body in heaven. I will not be in a chair. I sometimes have quite a bit of physical pain, it often makes me think of heaven where there will be no pain or tears, for anyone. Since I have accepted God as my Lord I have become a more patient person. The Bible encourages us to clothe ourselves with patience (*Col. 3 v 12*).

"In 1987, Mum, Dad and I went to California, during the holiday we stayed in Yosemite Valley, Yosemite National Park, High Sierra Mounts. I would say that Yosemite Valley was like a cathedral without a roof, and the mountains are the church organs. We drove to Glacier Point 7,214ft and had a panoramic vista of the valley and beyond, the scenery declaring God's majesty and creative power, the beauty of the scenery reinforced my faith in God. I said to myself, 'If you think this is beautiful what do you think Heaven will be like?' Nothing will be compared to it. Heaven will be heavenly and the Bible promises that we will enjoy God for ever.

"God refreshes the parts others cannot reach!!

"If we put our sins and anxieties at the foot of the cross of Jesus, after saying a prayer accepting the Lord as our saviour into our lives, we will receive spiritual healing and this will start us on the incredible eternal journey and adventure, and God will refresh us on this journey and inspire and encourage us. God is at work in my life creating something special and precious.

"Thank you for listening. God bless you all.

"CHRIST IS RISEN. HE IS RISEN INDEED HALLELUJAH".

After the service we all went to the vicarage for coffee; it was a beautiful sunny morning so we enjoyed our coffee in the garden. It looked very attractive – the trees were full of blossom and the birds were singing.

A few months later a man appeared at our door from Barrow Church, his name was Andrew Hunt. He had heard my testimony at Barrow and had come to ask for some advice on presenting his own testimony at a forthcoming mission to be held in the neighbouring village of Kelsall. Later I was invited to share the platform with Andrew at the same event held in a big top in August 1989. This I was pleased to do and we committed the event to the Lord in prayer. Prayer is vital in order to communicate with God and in September of that year an opportunity arose to meet in prayer triplets, that is, three people coming together for prayer. Our triplet met in my house and included an old friend, Tim Healy and Andrew Hunt. Five years later in 1995, Don Davies, a friend of Mum's from church, asked if I would like him to start a Bible Study group. This was good news, so we started right away. On our first study Don's wife, Val, came along together with another friend called Margaret, who became a Christian a short time ago. We have spent many happy hours sharing insight from God's word and experiences with people and we have continued to meet on a regular basis. Our first major study was the last book of the Bible, the Revelation of St. John the Divine, written while he was in exile on the Greek island of Patmos. This book is rich in symbolism and picture language. If you are thinking of reading the Bible for the first time, this is not the book to start with! However, when you do read this book of the Bible you will find the help of a commentary, such as William Barclay, invaluable. You could sum up the book of Revelation in three words, "Our God Reigns". The second major study was the gospel of Luke the Physician, a wonderful painter with words and clearly written for anyone to read and understand. It's an ideal book to begin a first study of the New Testament. Who knows what book we will study next?

Chapter 15

My 21st Birthday (Coming of Age)

On 10th May 1988, I got up early and as usual, read God's word, the Bible, Psalm 121 and Psalm 139. For breakfast we all had scrambled eggs and smoked salmon – my choice – which was delicious! I opened some fabulous presents, including a white tuxedo, winged collar shirt and red dicky bow together with matching cummerbund. Representatives from the Chester branch of the Muscular Dystrophy Group came around mid-morning with a box full of fruit and a music tape, which was much appreciated. Relatives had appeared by lunchtime, when we 'popped' a bottle of champers and canapés were enjoyed. We all had a good chat and a laugh. In the afternoon, after everyone had gone home to get ready for the evening session, my sister Christine and I read from a book given as a birthday gift entitled, *Songs of Light on the Psalms*, and some poetry from another book by Gordon Benningfield, called *Poems of the Countryside*.

It was soon time to slip into my tuxedo gear ready for the evening dinner 'n' disco at Mungo's Restaurant near the Oulton Park motor racing circuit. The restaurant overlooked Oulton Mill Pool, a fabulous setting in which we enjoyed crab and avocado salad for starters, followed by grapefruit and orange sorbet to cleanse the palate, before diving into a main course of veal with assorted vegetables followed by strawberries and cream or chocolate roulade. I chose the lighter of the two! After dinner came the inevitable speeches of thanks. I had

Me aged 19, pictured at home in Chester.

Me on my 21st birthday, resplendent in my new tuxedo!

my turn after Dad and here's what I said:

"I would just like to say first of all thank you for coming; I am glad you could all make it and thanks for the lovely cards and presents. I would like to thank Mum and Dad, Chris and all my friends and relatives for all their love and encouragement over the years. I would like to give a special thank you to Professor Edwards for his support – I will be eternally grateful. The best thing about the future is that it only comes one day at a time. Thanks again, enjoy yourselves."

After the speeches, all the guests proceeded upstairs to the dance floor. I followed afterwards, got into my electric chair and we danced the night away, wheel-a-boogie-woogie. The DJ tried to cater for everyone's tastes in music – or eras more like! The party had a fantastic family atmosphere and everyone seemed to get on well together. The climax of the evening was to sit in the middle of the dance floor circling around in my chair while everyone gathered around me to sing 'Auld Lang Syne' and 'For He's a Jolly Good Fellow'. It was quite overwhelming with all the presents and cards. A memorable 21st!

Chapter 16

First Trip to Canada, July 1988

This was the second time I had planned a major holiday itinerary so I had a good deal of previous experience to draw from. I also had the benefit of Grandad and Grandma who had been to this part of Canada.

We set off on our holiday to Vancouver on Canada's West coast, in July 1988, flying from Heathrow to Vancouver via Seattle. The flight time to Seattle was eight hours and five minutes and the final leg of the flight from Seattle took 30 minutes. The hotel we stayed at for the first couple of nights was Vancouver's Hyatt Regency. Our room gave us fabulous views of Stanley Park, the Lion Gate Bridge and the beautiful North Shore Mountains.

On our first full day we walked by the harbour before breakfast. It was a pleasant, sunny morning. We saw the Canada Place Complex, which included the Pan Pacific Hotel, a World Trade Centre and a cruise ship terminal, where a large liner was docked. The complex had five huge air-supported sails which looked spectacular. They were built for the Expo '86 event. After breakfast we strolled into the historic Gastown, the oldest remaining part of the original city of Vancouver, where we observed the world's first steam powered clock. There were many cannery buildings and brick sidewalks, which were flat and so ideal for the wheelchair. It was here we saw a statue of Jack Deighton, nicknamed, "Gassy" Jack. He was born in Hull, England, and was an explorer, pirate and one of the founding

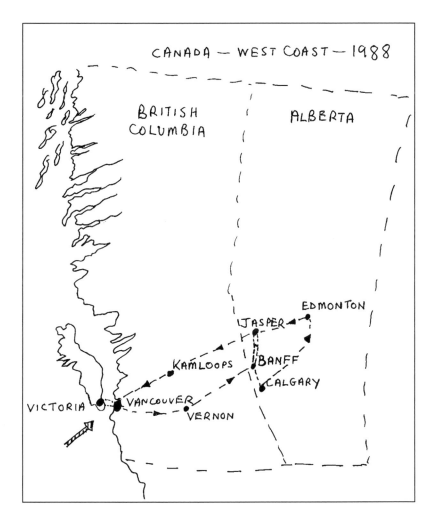

fathers' of Gastown, where he became famous for his Gassy monologues. We were able to go to the top of the Harbour Centre Tower in a glass lift and at the top, from the observation deck, had a 360 degree panoramic view of the city with a good views of the mountains including Grouse Mountain.

Later that morning we jumped into the car to visit Capilano Canyon, which is in north Vancouver. We travelled through

101

Stanley Park and over the Lion Gate Bridge, whose entrance is crowned by two lions. At the Capilano Canyon a suspension bridge spans the canyon which is 230ft deep. My mother started to walk on the bridge but soon made a hasty retreat as it started to swing with the weight of people, causing her heart to miss a beat! There are many fabulous trees in the canyon, such as Douglas firs, the largest growing tree in Canada. We saw a group of totem poles in the park and also watched an Indian in the process of carving one. We spotted two Canadian robins, which are bigger than our British robin. Next stop was Horseshoe Bay, going due west travelling on the Upper Levels Highway. There are many steep mountains here and in the centre of the bay is the tree-carpeted Gambier Island. Incidentally, from Horseshoe Bay, British Columbia Ferries sail to Vancouver Island.

We had our lunch at Horseshoe Bay, then travelled back to Vancouver and spent the rest of the day on board a boat which belonged to some friends. It was moored in the Thunderbird Marina, named after a mythical Indian bird: when it flew its wings darkened the sky, when its eyes flashed they were like lightning, and when its wings flapped it was like thunder. According to tribal legend, the Indians were inspired by this creature.

Once on board the boat my wheelchair was anchored down securely with rope. The boat had a 350 horsepower Buick engine, and was 36ft in length with six berths. It was a glorious warm sunny day as we sailed around Stanley Park and the Lion Gate Bridge and entered the Gulf of Georgia. We did some fishing but didn't have any luck because there was a seal swimming behind the boat who disturbed the fish! We sailed into English Bay and into False Creek, to sail around the Expo '86 site in which we saw the British Columbia Place Stadium, the world's largest air supported stadium. Made of Teflon, the roof covers an area of 10 acres with a seating capacity of 60,217.

We fed some Canada geese from the side of the boat. We carried on to Burrard Inlet to watch the Royal Princess cruise liner sail out of the dock on a ten-day cruise to Alaska. As we followed in the wake of the liner, out towards the Lion Gate Bridge, it made our boat rock from side to side – an exhilarating feeling. Another cruise ship sailed behind the Royal Princess to add to the swell but I managed to balance all right. Sea planes were taking off and landing all the time. We had a very pleasant meal on our friends' boat and it was a really enjoyable first day.

The following day we took a car ferry to Vancouver Island to visit Victoria, capital of British Columbia, sailing from Tsawwassen to Swartz Bay, which was a distance of 24 miles. Whilst we were waiting, six police cars zoomed past us to arrest someone disembarking from the ferry. After a few vehicles drove off, I saw two men in a car who looked rather suspicious. Suddenly, the police cars came after them with sirens blaring away; they surrounded the vehicle with guns drawn and captured the men and handcuffed them, all adding a little more excitement. Once on board the ferry we parked our car in a space designated a 'disabled spot' next to a lift which made things easier for us. The ferry sailed through the picturesque tree-carpeted gulf islands. After disembarking we proceeded on our journey to Victoria, which is named after Queen Victoria and became the capital of British Columbia in 1868. We strolled around the quaint inner harbour which Captain James Cook sailed into on his adventures in the Pacific region in 1778. The Parliament buildings which overlooked the harbour and yacht basin had turrets and a beautiful rotunda dome. We walked past the famous ivy-covered Empress Hotel, a Canadian Pacific Hotel. Some time later we strolled on to Bastion Square, the site where James Douglas of the Hudson Bay Fur Trading Company established Fort Victoria in 1843. On the pavement in Bastion Square there is a brass plaque inscribed with 'The Hudson Bay Fur Trading Company (and the company logo) formed in AD 1670'. After a light lunch, we went on to Thunderbird Park, famous for its collection of totem poles, most of them crested with carvings of the aforementioned mythical Thunderbird. A number of horse drawn carriages could be seen winding their way around Victoria. We drove to Beacon Hill Park, a massive park, well laid out with attractive flower beds, and lakes graced with a variety of ducks. In the park we saw one of the world's largest totem poles carved by an Indian chief called Mungo Martin. Close by, we looked across the Juan de Fuca Straits and saw the majestic snow-capped Olympic Mountains of Washington State, U.S.A.. Then we got the ferry back to the mainland and back to the City of Vancouver. The evening meal in our hotel, the Hyatt, was in the Fish and Co. restaurant. Next to our table a superb pianist, Jim Hodgkinson, played a wonderful range of music which made our evening all the more enjoyable.

Next day we travelled from Vancouver to Vernon in the south central interior of British Columbia. We drove over the mighty Fraser River in Port Coquitlam just outside the city of Vancouver, observing numerous logs floating down the river. Late in the morning we entered Manning Provincial Park which is a 70-mile roller-coaster ride that ascends from near sea level, beginning at Hope and climbing to the 4,500ft summit of Allison Pass with its beautiful mountain scenery and a crystal clear, fast flowing river called the Similkamean, which threads through part of the park. We saw lovely alpine meadows. Later we drove on through the Okanagan Valley, a famous fruit-growing area, where we came through a town called Penticton. The first orchard in the Okanagan valley was planted in 1874. The beautiful Okanagan and Skaha lakes are at the opposite ends of Penticton and offer vast expanses of shoreline, flanked by lovely mountains. Next-stop off was at Summerland which is surrounded by lush orchards and vineyards. The first commercial orchard in the Okanagan valley was planted here in 1890. We walked around a small fruit market and bought some juicy peaches, nectarines and apples to eat. Incidentally, there is a Loch Ness-type monster here in Lake Okanagan which the locals call "OgoPogo". At the northern end of Lake Okanagan where it narrows, we drove over a floating causeway to the town of Kelowna, which is the centre of the fruit, vegetable and vineyards industries in the Okanagan valley. One third of all apples grown in Canada are shipped from here.

We continued driving to Vernon, past Kalamalka Lake, which is an Indian name meaning "lake of many colours". We stayed at the Village Green Hotel, our base for the night, which had good facilities for wheelchairs making things easier to get around. We enjoyed a nice meal there, sampling a full-bodied Chenin Blanc wine from the nearby Mission Hill Winery. It certainly went down well! Later, we drove down to the shore of Lake Kalamalka to watch the sun setting. There were some nice properties around there.

We got on the road early the following day and set off from Vernon to Banff, in the Province of Alberta. As we travelled the mountains were getting higher and higher, and we went over the mighty Columbia River. Nearby was Mount Revelstoke National Park. We were now on the 5,000 mile long Trans-Canada Highway, which passes the south eastern portion of the Park. Mount Revelstoke Park has many sharp mountain peaks, this is the Western edge of the Selkirk mountain ranges. It is an area of awe-inspiring scenery, the work of the great artificer and Sovereign Creator. This road, called "Rogers Route," was open for automobiles in 1962. We carried on to Glacier National Park, where we observed a number of glaciers and snowfields. As we drove through, we saw a few snow sheds to protect the roads from avalanches. Twelve per cent of the Park is covered in perpetual snow and ice. This area became the scene of the 19th century battle between railroad engineers and the mountains when insurmountable difficulties had to be overcome because of the steep mountain walls, numerous slide areas and the weather. Avalanches reaching speeds of 200 mph tore up sections of railway track and left other sections buried in tons of snow. In 1910, 62 workers were killed by an avalanche as they worked to clear an earlier slide. Because of this, together with the mounting costs, it was decided to tunnel through Mt. McDonald. On the Trans-Canada highway similar obstacles were met as it crossed the pass, but the use of mobile howitzers to dislodge potential mountain slides and other methods of controlling avalanches, have held the road's position in the area.

We stopped off at Glacier National Park Lodge for refreshments and saw a huge glass showcase with two stuffed bears, a black bear and a grizzly – fabulous creatures. With spectacular mountains flanking us, with their beautiful snow covered peaks, words cannot express the glory of the scenery.

Some miles later we parked by the side of the muddy-coloured Columbia River and got a grand sweeping view of the mountains. I observed a beautiful black and white butterfly in this spot: 60 per cent of the butterfly population in Canada can be found in British Columbia. This richness is due to the diversity of terrain, from coastal cliffs to inland mountains. Yoho National Park (incidentally "Yoho" is a Cree Indian word meaning "astonishment") was a place we stopped off at. In the Park was Emerald Lake, it certainly was an amazing colour, with Burgess Mountain towering above it. On this mountain are the Burgess Shale fossil beds which are 500 million years old. These fossils describe in an unusual way the marine life that existed when the mountains were covered by the sea. There were lovely jagged mountains everywhere with lots of snow and ice covering them. Yoho National Park was named a World Heritage Site by the United Nations in 1985 because of its exceptional landscapes, including the Takakkaw

My pen and ink drawing of Burgess Mountain

Falls which plunge approximately 1,200 ft – an amazing height and sight and sound!

We travelled over the Kicking Horse Pass into Banff National

Park in Alberta and stopped off at Lake Louise, known as the "Jewel of the Canadian Rockies", where we walked through a wooded area with nice flat pavements. Chateau Lake Louise Hotel overlooks the lake, and the hotel gardens are beautifully laid out with lovely vivid red Icelandic poppies. We saw the majestic Victoria Glacier at one end of the turquoise lake. The colour is due to glacial sediments and rock flour flowing into the lake. I enjoyed a delicious maple-flavoured ice cream here.

We stayed in Banff Rocky Mountain Resort for two nights, nestled in its valley of green meadows and pine forests at the base of Mount Rundle and Cascade Mountain. There were lots of Columbian ground squirrels frolicking around.

The following morning as Dad went outside to take a photo of Mum, some people were trying to attract his attention to tell him about a bear which was at the back of the hotel. Dad rushed to find the bear, which was sharpening his claws on a tree, and succeeded in getting a good photograph of him. I missed the bear by 30 seconds but saw his tracks – it was most exciting. We visited the Banff Springs Hotel which was owned by the Canadian Pacific Railway and built in 1883, and had a good look round. It had a fabulous banqueting hall with lovely chandeliers, a minstrels' gallery, wooden panelling and a grand piano. Strolling on to the red terrace we had a panoramic vista of the Sundance range of snowy capped mountains, the Bow River Valley and Banff Springs golf course. We travelled on to see the lovely Bow Falls nearby where the sound of cascading water was music to the ears. As we drove on to the Bow River Parkway, a quieter alternative to the Trans-Canada Highway, the castellated peaks of Castle Mountain dominated the view from the Parkway. We stopped off at Johnston Canyon and walked to the canyon's lower falls waterfall. While we were on the walk to the falls you could see tree roots and small rocks sticking up all over the place. There were steep slopes in parts, making it a very bumpy ride in my wheelchair.

Lovely shafts of golden sunlight streamed through the canyon together with a turbulent and beautiful blue-green river which also threaded its way along the canyon. When we reached the side of the waterfall we went into a small cave. There was an opening at the end about two feet from the waterfall where you could feel the spray from the falls.

We proceeded on to Moraine Lake in the valley of the Ten Peaks, with glaciers on the peaks. The lake was bright turquoise, which looked resplendent in the sunlight and there were also lots of beautiful alpine flowers.

We drove up through Banff National Park on Highway 93, referred to as the Ice Fields Parkway, which derives its name from the chain of ice fields lying alongside the continental divide and is the source of many rivers draining into the Pacific, Atlantic and the Arctic Oceans via Hudson Bay. We had a picnic overlooking the grandeur of Crow Foot Glacier, a hanging glacier which resembles a crow's foot. At the bottom of the glacier lies another lovely turquoise lake with innumerable Douglas firs.

Next stop off was Peyto, named after Bill Peyto, explorer and pioneer. As we drove to a special car park near the lake viewpoint, I spotted a Clark's nutcracker bird. The lake is located in the Mistaya Valley. You could see the glacial sediment clearly flowing into it as well as the fabulously sculpted mountains encircling us and an enormous amount of snow and ice.

At the Saskatchewan River crossing we came out of the Banff National Park into the Rocky Mountain Forest Reserve, and drove to Abraham Lake, named after a Stoney Indian. At one end of the lake is Bighorn Dam which was built in 1972. We saw a number of mountain sheep strolling across the highway. I thought the mountain air might affect my breathing but everything was all right. As we travelled back to Banff the lofty mountains were spectacular to behold. Once back at our base in Banff I had a pleasant refreshing swim and Jacuzzi in the

My pen and ink drawing of Moraine Lake
in the Valley of the Ten Peaks

hotel pool, before we drove into the town to have a meal of succulent prime rib of beef. After the meal I had a walk around, looking at the Sundance range of mountains surrounding the town, another wondrous scene.

Next day we travelled from Banff to Calgary. Before leaving

Banff we visited Lake Minnewanka which is a Stoney Indian word meaning, "water spirit". It's a lovely lake encircled by enormous, awesome mountains and carpets of beautiful Douglas fir trees. We drove through a place called Canmore, where the cross-country and biathlon events of the 1988 Winter Olympics had been staged earlier in the year at the Canmore Nordic Centre, located on the lower slopes of the dramatic Mount Rundle.

We drove into Kananaskis country to see the Nakiska ski hill at Mount Allan where the alpine events of the Olympics were organised. *Nakiska* is a Cree Indian word meaning "to meet". On display we saw the flags representing the 26 countries participating in the Olympics. There was also a sign that said "Beware of grizzly bears" - if you see a bear you are expected to report it to a Park Ranger. Kananaskis village, at an elevation of 5,000ft, is a few miles up the road from the Nakiska ski hill. The village was built by the Canadian Pacific Railway Company and comprises the Kananaskis Lodge with exclusive shops and information centre, an attractive large pond with a waterfall at one end and beautiful trees planted all around the place. A lot of wood has been used in the construction of the buildings in keeping with the environment. We had a light lunch here of clam chowder in a restaurant overlooking the majestic mountains.

We set off once again on our travels to Calgary, whose history traces back to 1875, when a contingent of scarlet-coated Northwest Mounted Police (the forerunners of the Royal Canadian Mounted Police) pitched their tents at the confluence of the Bow and Elbow Rivers and set up Fort Calgary. We continued driving to Calgary stopping off at the Olympic Park on the outskirts of the city, where the bobsleigh and luge runs and ski jumps are located. This is where the British competitor "Eddie the Eagle" did his famous 90-metre jump in the 1988 Olympics.

We stayed in Calgary that night. After unloading our baggage in our room, we wandered around the town and visited Devonian Gardens on the 4th floor of Toronto Dominion Square. It is a relaxing garden paradise with waterfalls, fountains, pools, statues and 20,000 plants, of 138 varieties. The gardens cover an area of two hectares and there is a mile of walkways. All the shops and offices in Calgary are linked up by enclosed walkways which enable people to walk around the city in the middle of winter without warm gloves, scarves and so on. We had dinner in the Calgary Towers revolving restaurant, called the Panorama Room. The tower is 626ft high. We had a delicious meal coupled with a wonderful view of the city's landmarks such as the 60-acre Stampede Park, home of the world-famous Calgary exhibition and stampede. We could also see where the Northwest Mounted Police had set up Fort Calgary and a small square in which the Olympic competitors received their medals. The snow-clad Rocky Mountains looked magnificent in the distance.

We travelled on from Calgary to Edmonton on Highway 2. As we left Calgary we drove through part of Chinatown, where Chinese immigrants who came to Western Canada to work on the railroad stayed in Calgary to set up restaurants, shops, businesses and other kinds of employment. On the journey to Edmonton we passed through a lot of farmland where we saw fields of wheat and maize and observed some beautiful ranches with many cattle. I spotted a bird of prey – I'm not sure what it was, but the sighting was exciting nevertheless. Another sighting which caught my eye was a white wooden church by the roadside, just like the ones you see in a Western movie set! We stopped off for refreshment at a place called Red Deer which took its present name from the Cree Indian translation (*Waskasoo Seepee*) which describes the abundance of deer found in the river valley and surrounding areas. Red Deer is Alberta's major centre for conventions and meetings and has lots of lush green areas. The next town we travelled through was Leduc, near Edmonton, it was hereabouts in 1947 that a strike of oil brought about a petrol-boom and quickly established Calgary as the Canadian petroleum industry's corporate head office and financial centre. It's now the oil capital of Canada. We saw the characteristic flame stacks associated with oil refining.

In Edmonton, the capital of Alberta, we visited West Edmonton Mall, which at the time was the world's largest shopping, amusement and entertainment complex. It comprised 800 shops, 110 eating places and 34 cinemas. There were a couple of tigers in cages on the floor below us which were brought out for people to have their photograph taken with, so I couldn't resist going to see them. I stroked the larger tiger which was 12 weeks old. It was too big to sit on my lap so I had the smaller nine-week-old tiger cub called "Cringer". They were magnificent creatures. There was also a large aviary full of beautiful birds such as the Secretary Bird. Other amenities in the Mall included a large ice rink, a fair and a water park with a large enclosed water slide going into an enormous swimming pool with a wave machine. There was a submarine ride in a huge tank and close by, a pool with two dolphins swimming around. We passed some fountains which were actually brass trumpets with water shooting up out of them, which was a rather unusual design.

Edmonton is the Gateway to the North and is famous for its parks which stretch for miles in its lush green Saskatchewan River Valley. Edmonton served as one of the major stepping off points for the Klondike Gold Rush. Our visit coincided with the "Klondike Festival" which is held every July for 10 days. In our hotel lobby there was a display to celebrate the festival, comprising a screen which announced in large letters, "The Klondike Days". In a glass cabinet was a bust of a woman from the Klondike Gold Rush era which began in 1898. There was also a piece of railway track and a waxwork model of a woman dressed in the attire of that period. As we walked to the Chateau Lacombe Hotel's revolving restaurant called "La Ronda" a lady walked across the street in Klondike period costume including an elegant parasol. As my main course in the restaurant I had Arctic char coated with saffron. Delicious! It tasted to me rather like salmon. From the revolving restaurant we saw the four glass pyramidal structures of Muttart Conservatory, the John Ducey Stadium, the beautiful North Saskatchewan River and some oil refineries.

We travelled to Jasper the next day on Yellowhead Highway 16. Before leaving Edmonton we drove to the legislative capitol building, an elegant monument to Alberta's early builders constructed between 1907-12 in terracotta with a fabulous rotunda dome. We then continued driving on Highway 16 to Jasper, through a lot of farmland with fabulous ranches and numerous cattle grazing the flat land. About 70 miles outside Jasper the landscape became more mountainous. We turned off the Yellowhead Highway onto the Miette Hot Springs Road. A short distance down the road we stopped off at Punchbowl Falls which are about 30 miles east of Jasper. I could not see the falls because the terrain was too difficult to get the wheelchair down to see them, so Dad video-ed them for me. We travelled to the end of Miette Springs Road, where there was a swimming pool which has natural sulphur water pumped into it from the nearby mountain spring. We saw a bird of prey that looked like a hawk, but I am not sure what type. It was a thrilling sight nonetheless! A number of mountain sheep wandered across the road. We were looking for Miette Roche Mountain, but could not find it because it was draped with a curtain of cloud. It was not until we had turned around to retrace our steps back to the main Highway 16 that we glimpsed a section of the mountain. The scenery was awe-inspiring, indescribable.

We turned off the Yellowhead Highway just outside the town site of Jasper onto the Jasper Park Lodge Road and then onto Maligne Road leading down to Maligne Lake. We had lunch at the Maligne Canyon Teahouse overlooking the 165ft deep limestone canyon which is a dramatic example of the eroding power of water. It is a beautiful canyon, but the terrain was a bit rough in parts which made it a little difficult for the wheelchair. We drove onto Maligne Lake and passed Medicine Lake which was a lovely turquoise. The lake's water level fluctuates from season to season due to an underground drainage system. The medicine men used to tell their fellow Indians that it was they who controlled the water level of the lake. The road we travelled on terminated at the edge of Maligne Lake which is located in Maligne Valley and lies a mile above sea level in a basin created by mountains soaring over 10,000ft. It is the largest glacier-fed lake in the Canadian Rockies and is 14 miles long. The western film *Rosemary* was filmed here in 1939 and there is a boat-house in which a boat used in the film was kept. We travelled on to our hotel in Jasper, the Lobstick Lodge, for a couple of nights. Lobsticks were markers on early trails in the mountains made by lobbing off the branches of trees on the trails, often showing rendezvous points and items of interest.

We drove into the town of Jasper and walked around. There was a nice tourist office in an old log cabin, with lovely flower beds and lawns, where we picked up lots of information. Jasper nestles in the Athabasca River Valley, and is named after Jasper Hawes who trapped here in the early 1800s. Towering above the town of is Mt. Edith Cavell. After our evening meal we drove near to the foot of Whistler's Mountain (elevation 7,000 ft), and saw a male elk with its huge antlers resting in the undergrowth – it was a magnificent specimen. As we watched the sun setting overlooking a wide part of the mighty Athabasca River, it was an awesome sight with the mountains and a vast sea of beautiful trees. It was so tranquil that I felt at one with nature.

The following day we travelled through the Jasper National Park. Our first port of call was the spectacular Athabasca Falls produced where the Athabasca River is funnelled through a steep gorge. We felt the spray from these falls and the fabulous mountain grandeur surrounding us. Later we passed Stutfield Glacier, an excellent example of a braided river, and saw the beautiful blue hue on the ice caused by the air in the glacier. Next stop-off was Athabasca Glacier in the Columbia ice fields – the largest accumulation of snow and ice south of the Arctic. Having parked the car about five feet from the foot of the magnificent glacier I watched Mum and Dad walk to the edge and on to it. There was quite a lot of cloud about but it was fascinating watching the cloud lift off the snow-clad mountains.

A glacier is a slow-moving river of ice which goes through cycles of advancing and melting each year. There was an enormous amount of sand, gravel and rocks strewn over the valley floor from mountain slides and the glacier melting. You can journey on a snow coach with special, enormous wheels on to the glacier.

We stopped for refreshments at the Columbia Ice Fields Chalet, entering through a back door to avoid a flight of steps, which was easier for us. Once inside, whilst I was drinking a marmot appeared under the table – much to my amazement and amusement!

We continued travelling through the Jasper National Park and as we drove over the Sunwapta Pass, a spectacular pass with an elevation of over 7,000ft, we observed a few fantastic waterfalls which were really dramatic. Sunwapta Pass marks the boundary between Jasper and Banff National Park. We parked the car in a small lay-by to take some pictures of the Sunwapta Pass and to admire the incredible scenery. A short time later, outside the pass, we came off the main highway and into a gap between the trees to enjoy a picnic lunch in a pleasant spot on a bend of the Sunwapta River – it was very peaceful there in the eerie silence with nobody else around. Then we slowly made our way back to Jasper and stopped off at a car park in the forest to see the Sunwapta Falls. Here, the Sunwapta River abruptly changes course from north west to south west and drops into a deep canyon producing very powerful falls. Just before the waterfall there is an island full of evergreen trees towering over 200ft high. We walked along the canyon wall for a short distance – it was very bumpy with tree roots everywhere. Dad pushed me down a steep slope then on to a bridge overlooking the waterfall and canyon, where the noise of the waterfall was music to the ears.

Then we travelled on towards Edith Cavell Mountain, turning off the main Highway 93 onto the 93A, an access road which took us past the Athabasca Falls giving us a view from a different angle The road became very narrow and steep in parts with many hairpin bends. At one point we stopped the car, briefly, on the roadside and had a glorious panoramic view of the snow-capped mountains flanking us. We passed many fabulous evergreens, cedars and Douglas fir trees. A short time later we observed Edith Cavell Lake through the trees – an emerald lake in a most beautiful setting. Towering above the lake was the splendid Edith Cavell Mountain with an elevation of over 11,000ft. On the north east face of the mountain is Angel Glacier. The mountain was named after a British nurse, Edith Cavell, who was executed by the Germans in 1915 for aiding the escape of Allied troops from Belgium. Mum and Dad walked down to Edith Cavell Lake – the terrain was rather rough and therefore not suitable for wheelchairs. Later we drove to the Jasper Park Lodge which is located two miles outside the town of Jasper and saw a group of deer as they walked across the road. Upon entering the Jasper Park Lodge we passed a large duck pond. People stay in log cabins here and among the facilities are a golf course and riding stables. The

My pen and ink drawing of Mount Edith Cavell

main building overlooks scenic Lake Beauvert, another beautiful emerald lake with reflections of the lovely scenery. We saw
a few people canoeing on the lake in twin Indian-style kayaks.
Mount Edith Cavell and Whistler's Mountain top terminal for
the cable car were clearly visible.

Next day we travelled from Jasper to Kamloops on the
Yellowhead Highway, coming out of the province of Alberta
into British Columbia and into Mount Robson Provincial Park.
As we came through the Yellowhead Pass, majestic snow-
capped mountains flanked us. We passed Moose Lake which
had beautiful reflections of the mountains and trees, where
sometimes moose can be spotted near the lake in the water
logged meadows – unfortunately we didn't see any ourselves.
We spent some time at Mount Robson, the highest mountain in
the Canadian Rockies, at 12,972ft it is a spectacular snow
capped mountain. It was fascinating to watch the cloud lifting
off this mountain.

Next stop-off was Mount Terry Fox Provincial Park, named
after Terry Fox, the man who had his leg amputated due to
cancer but ran the arduous 5,500 miles Trans-Canada Highway
to raise funds for cancer sufferers and raised 30 million dollars.
Sadly he was 1,600 miles from completing the run when the
cancer spread to his lungs and he died in 1981. Even though he
did not complete his run Terry gave countless cancer sufferers
hope and encouragement. Three months later a memorial was
unveiled in his memory at this spot. I saw the Terry Fox film,
Marathon of Hope, before going on this holiday.

A number of miles further south we observed a majestic
mountain soaring to the heavens with a tremendous amount of
snow on its slopes. We passed a beautiful waterfall and
stopped off at Dutch Lake in a place called Clearwater – it was
a picturesque lake with a carpet of lovely pink and white water
lilies. We spotted a number of Canada geese by the lake shore.
It was here I had a delicious small blueberry ice cream, but

even the small ice cream was generous! We then followed the course of the torrential North Thompson River for many miles. Miners from the east of Canada came down this river into Kamloops to the Cariboo gold rush. Kamloops is in a glacial cut valley flanked by hills and majestic mountains, has a semi-desert atmosphere and the climate here is rated one of the best in Canada. Incidentally, it is the tournament capital of British Columbia. We observed many houses high up on the hillsides. We spent one night in Kamloops (pronounced Kaloops by the Canadians) and our hotel room had a panoramic vista of the area. We strolled into a downtown shopping mall, and saw a beautiful tiger, a black panther, an adult leopard and two leopard cubs a few weeks old in cages. This was part of a wildlife survival project to heighten public awareness. There are nice flat sidewalks with trees dotted about the place. We went back to the hotel for a swim and spent time in the Jacuzzi which had powerful water jets. For dinner that evening I had a succulent steak, which was delicious!

The following day we travelled back to Vancouver on the Yellowhead Highway, the Coquihalla Highway and Highway 1. We drove to Riverside Park where the North and South Thompson Rivers converge. There's a beautifully laid-out park with many fabulous trees and flowers. We saw a marvellous old steam train on its track in the park. We intended to see the *Wanda Sue* sternwheeler paddle boat, but we didn't see it because it wasn't at the boat terminal. We found out that the boat owner had it moored at his home further up the river. Sternwheelers like this one originally explored the Thompson river in the 1800s and carried rails for the construction of the Canadian Pacific Railway. We then continued on our way back to Vancouver – it was quite a climb out of Kamloops giving a panoramic view over the city. We came through a lot of farmland with majestic vistas of the mountains.

The next leg of the journey was on the Coquihalla Highway

which comes over the mountains and had been opened the previous year, 1987. The scenery was awe-inspiring, with the snow capped mountains surrounding us and the crystal clear Coquihalla River threading its way through the area. We went through a number of snow sheds built with reinforced concrete which protect the road from avalanches. We stopped off at the site of the Hope landslide which occurred in 1965 when the side of Johnston Peak collapsed sending 46 million tons of rock over the Highway. The slide was caused by a minor tremor and a few people were killed as they travelled in their cars.

Later we had a drive-in McDonald's meal at a place called Chilliwack – a very quick, efficient service and a new experience for me. Our burgers were ready in 30 seconds!

We spent three nights back in Vancouver at the end of our Canadian holiday. I observed a black squirrel running up the hotel porter's legs and then scampering up the hotel steps and so putting on quite a show! Our hotel room had a veranda – on one side of it you could see English Bay and on the other side the spectacular North Shore Mountains. I sunbathed overlooking English Bay watching the seagulls gliding, diving and soaring accompanied by a tape by Neil Diamond, called *Jonathan Livingston Seagull* on my Walkman. I also relaxed watching the people windsurfing, cruising in pleasure boats and generally enjoying themselves. Later that evening, after our meal we walked to our friends' apartment which overlooked English Bay and were able to watch a fantastic sunset over the bay. Later that evening back at our hotel Mum and I took the lift to the restaurant to get a panoramic view of Vancouver's skyline: the Lion Gate Bridge and downtown Vancouver looked magical lit up.

The following day was a Sunday so Mum and I and two friends went to a Methodist Church close to the hotel to quite an informal church service. Everyone was very friendly and made us most welcome. Later, we drove around the 1,000-acre

Stanley Park, passing the lagoon with an attractive fountain. A colony of Canada geese was sunbathing by the lagoon. A short time later we observed the Royal Vancouver Yacht Club, Deadman's Island, which was an Indian burial ground, and Totem Pole Park, with its large collection of totems carved by the coastal Indians. Before leaving the Park we passed Prospect Point with its fabulous view of the North Shore Mountains and the Lion Gate Bridge. For our evening meal we drove due West of Vancouver to Horseshoe Bay to the Boathouse restaurant. We sat on the balcony overlooking the bay, with Gambier Island in the centre and the sheer mountains looking absolutely fantastic. We watched a number of ferries coming in and out of Horseshoe Bay. For dinner, we started with shared a platter of fried squid and fried Camembert, fried chicken and spare ribs, all of which could be dipped into four different kinds of sauce. For the main course I had thresher shark cooked teriyaki style and very meaty – a fabulous culinary delight! After the meal and a short stroll in the lovely evening light around Horseshoe Bay, we drove to nearby Whytecliff Park and saw some superb mansions on the cliff and numerous trees surrounding them. Bald Eagles nest in the heights of Whytecliff Park but we were unable to see any on this visit. Once back in Vancouver, we stopped to see if our friends were at home, but they weren't so we drove on a little way and caught up with them on an evening walk. They jumped into the car with us and gave us a conducted tour of the park. The lagoon we had seen earlier looked particularly beautiful with its reflections of the evening summer sky. The crowning glory of the evening coupled with the magnificent sunset was the spotting of a racoon in bushes at the roadside.

The next day we visited the Bloedel Conservatory in Queen Elizabeth Park which marks the geographic centre of Vancouver atop the 500ft Little Mountain. This conservatory is a dome-shaped structure of 1,490 Plexiglas bubble panels.

My pen and ink drawing of a racoon

Housed inside the dome is a tropical oasis of exotic tropical plants and flowers with a hundred, equally exotic, free flying birds. While we were there a wedding party was having photographs taken. People often use the park to record their wedding day in this beautiful setting. Also here two former quarries have been transformed into picturesque Japanese ornamental gardens with many flowers, trees and shrubs. From this location, set high up, we enjoyed a coffee and cakes coupled with an excellent view over the Vancouver skyline.

Later we travelled through Vancouver's Chinatown, which possesses the largest Chinese community outside mainland China. We passed the absolutely massive Canada Place Stadium. Chinatown's entrance was a highly decorated and colourful type of archway. Some of the buildings had a lot of character, and even the telephone kiosks have pagoda-shaped roofs. We saw vegetable and fruit markets and shops selling Chinese curios, such as lanterns and door chimes. We drove on to the Pan Pacific Hotel complex at Canada Place, where the interior design of the hotel appeared a little bare, that is, lacking in decoration and ornamentation in favour of a minimalist flavour. However, water cascades and a few nice shops added 'splashes' of colour! We strolled onto the terrace by the air supported sails, a prominent design feature of the complex.

Later that evening, after sunbathing overlooking English Bay, we went to Trader Vic's Polynesian-style restaurant in which we had a fabulous Chinese meal – strange, but true!

Next day, our last day, we visited Granville Island – a little used industrial area which has now been transformed into an area with beautiful shops, restaurants, fish and vegetable markets, craft stalls and art galleries We went to our friends Clara and Ernest's apartment for a 'delivered to the door' pizza lunch and later set off for the airport and the flight home, at the end of a happy holiday.

Chapter 17

Sixth Trip to America and Second to Canada, June 1989

In June 1989, when I was 22, we went off to America and Canada again. It was the third time I had planned a major holiday so I was now really into the planning mode! Once more I had the benefit of my grandparents' help and advice.

A taxi took us to Manchester Airport where our plane was due to take off at 1.30pm. The plane was to fly from Gatwick, collecting passengers in Manchester en route to New York's J.F.K. Airport. However, there was a problem because the cargo door would not close, so they had to get a replacement door ordered and fitted. We ended up being delayed for eight hours, three hours of which were spent in Manchester, then the airport authorities then decided to fly us to Gatwick on a Jumbo that had just come into Manchester from Islamabad smelling of curry! We boarded the plane to New York at about 8.30pm then we had to wait until one of the pilots had made his way through the Gatwick traffic, so we finally took off at 9.30pm. We travelled in comfort, being up-graded to first class. We had a very nice meal and we managed to sleep well – there is so much more space in first class seats which also makes it easier to lift me in and out.

Eventually we arrived in New York around 11.30pm American time, picked up a hire car and drove to our hotel. We travelled over the Triborough Bridge and I told Dad to make a

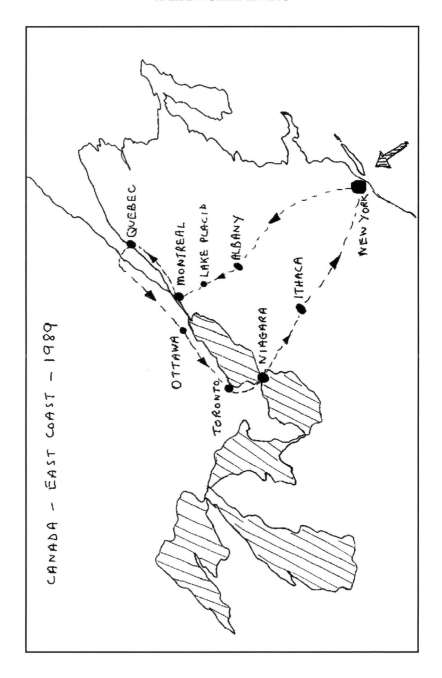

right turn, but he went left and we ended up in Harlem, a rough area of New York. We saw a group of people trying to break into a shop, which was quite frightening. However, we quickly managed to get on to the correct road and eventually arrived at the Grand Hyatt on 42nd Street Park Avenue at 1.30am. Because we were late the only room available was a Plaza Suite which was more like an apartment, with good facilities and plenty of space and quite luxurious.

After a good night's kip we enjoyed a leisurely breakfast at the sun garden restaurant in the hotel – you can't beat an American breakfast! Afterwards we hailed a yellow cab to take us to Washington Square, Greenwich Village. Many of the buildings in Washington Square had Ionic porticos which reflect the mid-19th century rage for Greek revivalism. Washington Square is the focal point of Greenwich Village, there is an attractive arch here and a lovely fountain. The streets of the village are lined with craft and curio shops, and art galleries. We walked on into Soho, passing many more art galleries and into Little Italy where there were some nice cafés and restaurants. Outside one restaurant there was a row of beautiful bay trees. It was here that I had a nice cool refreshing drink, which was most welcome on a very hot day. There were many souvenir shops and food stores displaying delicious fare. Nearby we saw the Manhattan Brewing Company with its lovely wrought iron gate entrance and a huge vat protruding out of the building. An Englishman set up this brewing company.

Later, we strolled into Chinatown where there was a lovely Chinese temple style building with a green tiled roof. In 1882 federal law excluded Chinese immigrants but in the 1960s racial restrictions were raised. The telephone kiosks had pagoda style roofs, like the ones in Vancouver. We walked into the South Tower of the Twin Towers of the World Trade Centre and took the lift to the enclosed observation deck on the 107th floor, towering 1,300 feet high. From here we had a wonderful panoramic view of New York taking in such landmarks as the lady herself, alias, the Statue of Liberty, Ellis Island, Manhattan Bridge and the famous Brooklyn Bridge with its Gothic granite towers and spidery gables of woven steel.

We strolled into Wall Street, the financial district of New York, passing the famous New York Stock Exchange, which has a Neo-Grecian facade. The street itself is narrow and the buildings are so tall that it's like a canyon. This is where all the financial action is. Close by, just across the road outside the Federal Hall National Memorial Building, is a statue of George Washington, standing where he made his vows of office in 1789.

We stopped to have a picnic lunch in Battery Park having picked up our sandwiches from a nearby Deli Bar; they were a meal in themselves, absolutely delicious and the size of a bus! In the park a dozen or so grey squirrels were putting on quite a show, scampering, jumping and generally frolicking about! A chap in the park was playing some very nice relaxing music on an electric organ, which added to the atmosphere. Another guy entertained us by fire-eating. Nearby, we observed a war memorial for World War Two comprising a large copper eagle on a plinth, in front of which stood a number of erect stone slabs inscribed with the names of those who had died in action – a fitting tribute. In the evening, after having a pleasant meal, we strolled into the Marriott Marquis Hotel and went into a glass elevator to "The View" revolving restaurant and bar – the only revolving restaurant in the city. We spent some time there enjoying the wonderful sights, such as the Empire State Building, the Chrysler Building and some other skyscrapers which were being built.

Next day we drove to Albany, the State capital of New York, and came through the Catskill Mountains. It was very pleasant scenery, with gentle rolling mountains where bald eagles spend the winter. We observed numerous lakes with lovely, mirrored reflections. There were lots of holiday homes here in the Catskills, many in keeping with the surrounding scenery. We spotted several waterfalls, one of which was particularly impressive, called Kaaterskill Falls, which plunged into a deep wooded gorge.

We arrived in Albany around 2pm and after checking in at our hotel for the night, walked around the Empire State Plaza, a futuristic complex of State Government Buildings centred on the massive State Capitol Buildings. I had planned to go up to the Corning Building's observation deck, but it had just closed for the night. Thankfully, an official on hearing we were tourists from the UK, kindly opened up the lift for us, escorted us up to the observation floor and pointed out various sites, such as the Mansion of the Governor of New York (at that time a man called Mario Cuomo), the University Buildings, a beautiful edifice which was a replica of the Cloth Guild Hall from Ypres in Belgium and the Hudson River.

The following day we drove on from Albany to Lake Placid in the Adirondacks National Park. On the way, just outside Saratoga Springs, as we were driving down the road we were stopped by two policemen, one wielding a large rifle and the other one showing a photograph of an escaped prisoner. They asked if we had seen him and said if we did we must report the sighting. They thought the suspect was lurking in nearby woods. We travelled alongside Lake George, the Queen of the American Lakes. The lake is 32 miles long and at the southern end of the lake there are 200 tree carpeted islands. We stopped off at the fabulous Sagamore resort, a colonial style hotel which had been recently restored to its former glory. It is located on an island with lots of greenery where we saw some fabulous speed boats and cruisers.

There are many beautiful houses on the lake shore with gorgeous sun decks on stilts. The road became rather steep and winding in places. We stopped once again at a view point, and observed Black Mountain rising majestically to 2,600ft. Later on, we came through a lot of farmland and then a portion of Lake Champlain came into view, which is an amazing 107 miles long. In 1609 the French explorer Samuel de Champlain discovered this lake and believed he saw a Loch Ness type monster in it. On the opposite side of the lake is the State of Vermont. We drove through the town of Keene, which is close to the high peaks of the Adirondacks National Park. The mountains flanking us were fantastic with their numerous trees and we also passed many lakes and ponds in this area. Lake Placid, our base for the night, hosted the 1980 Winter Olympics. At Mount Van Hovenburg we saw the refrigerated bobsleigh and luge run and cross country trails and passed the Olympic jumping complex, where the 70 and 90 metre ski-jumps took place.

Next stop-off was the Adirondacks Visitor Centre at a place called Paul Smith's, which had been opened the previous month. The visitor centre building complemented the natural environment. We were surrounded by lovely fragrant pine trees. As we walked on the terrace of the centre, it overlooked some marshes and we spotted a great blue heron and a wild rabbit. The scenery was spectacular, declaring God's glory and creative power.

Our hotel in the town of Lake Placid was set high on a hill and from our room we could see the majestic Whiteface Mountain towering above the waters of Lake Placid and Mirror Lake. Close to our hotel was the Olympic Centre – the largest ice complex of its kind in the world. It was the site of the U.S.A.'s miraculous ice hockey victory over the Soviet Union in the Winter Olympics of 1980.

The following morning after breakfast, while Mum and Dad were packing our car, I sat in the hotel car park and watched the early morning mist rising above Mirror Lake, a truly wonderful sight. A contrasting sight was a group of motor bikes, huge and powerful machines, some of which were towing mini-trailers brightly-decorated with landscape scenes and more abstract designs. I chatted briefly to one of the bikers who said they had travelled 500 miles the previous day and had a sore posterior to prove it! I'm not surprised, I have had the same problem.

Once packed, we were on our travels again and set off for Whiteface Mountain driving alongside the Ausable River for a few miles with its many raging rapids and large boulders. We passed the Whiteface Mountain Ski Centre, then travelled on Veterans Memorial Highway, a seven-mile toll road, to near the summit of Whiteface Mountain. A roller-coaster ride took us to a parking area 250ft below the summit of the mountain. To get to the top we proceeded through a tunnel to a lift which ascended through a shaft to the summit. From the summit, at an elevation of 4,876ft, we had a fantastic view of Lake Placid and the high peaks of the Adirondacks – a majestic view and awe-inspiringly beautiful. The weather was warm but a little hazy. Mosquitoes tried to attack me but I fought them when they came in reach of my deadly spitting ability. You certainly can't criticise my methods as it did the trick on this occasion!

Our next stop-off, the Ausable Chasm, was formed a staggering 500 million years ago. I was only able to see part of the gorge from the wheelchair from a small bridge which spanned the chasm. From this point we could see the brink of Rainbow Falls surging with power and Horseshoe Falls in the distance The erosive power of water is simply amazing. Incidentally, the Ausable Chasm empties into Lake Champlain, the sixth largest fresh water lake in America. We then crossed the American border into the Dominion of Canada. It took us 40 minutes to get through customs before travelling on to Montreal, which stands on the mighty St. Lawrence River. From one of the main bridges on the approach road we had a good view of the

Montreal skyline.

In 1535 the French explorer Jack Cartier landed in Montreal and he named a small mountain here, Park Mount Royal, in honour of the King of France, Francis I, and erected a cross atop of the mountain. Nearby we observed the famous St. Joseph's Oratory, one of Quebec's oldest shrines to the patron Saint of Canada. As we drove around Park Mount Royal, we parked the car at a viewpoint overlooking the city, so we could see such sites as the Olympic Park which hosted the games of 1976. The main stadium had a retractable roof. We also viewed the St. Lawrence River which the Indians call "the road that walks". Then we drove on to our hotel, the Bonaventure Hilton, where our room overlooked the Mary Queen of the World Basilica, a scaled-down replica of St. Peter's in Rome.

Montreal has a huge underground shopping city, which was built because of the very severe winter conditions experienced here. Later, we strolled into the old town and visited the Notre Dame Basilica, a neo-Gothic building which was richly decorated and whose organ is one of America's most powerful. The Basilica also contained wonderful stained glass windows, a number of paintings and an altar adorned with gold. Out in the streets were horse-drawn carriages. We walked into Jack Cartier Place, one of the oldest market places in Montreal, which had lots of cobblestoned streets that were nice to look at, but not very good for the wheelchair! The buildings here had a lot of style and character.

We had a look at the Port of Montreal and enjoyed a delicious meal in an open air French restaurant – it was a pleasant atmosphere with the birds chirping away.

We travelled from Montreal to Quebec and on the journey out of Montreal saw the Island of Il'e Notre Dame on the St. Lawrence River, which was the site of the Expo '67 exhibition. The geodesic dome was clearly visible from the car as we travelled by. This island is the venue for the Montreal Formula One

Right: paintings on stone of a linnet, goldcrest, great-tit and serin;

Below: paintings on stone of a kingfisher, American widgeon and long tailed duck.

g

Me with my sister Christine and my friend Edward

h

Grand Prix. Further on the journey we saw lots of farmland and areas for skiing. Along the road there were signs reading "Beware of moose", but we didn't spot any.

Just outside Quebec, at a place called Charny, we saw a set of waterfalls called "Chûtes de Chaudière", a spectacular sight. We were able to drive near to the waterfalls to get a good view, but couldn't see all the cascades as it was difficult ground for the wheelchair. We crossed over the St. Lawrence River on Pierre Laporte Road Bridge, into Quebec City. Close by is the Quebec Railway Bridge. In my opinion the bridges are reminiscent of Scotland's Forth Road Bridge and Railway Bridge. Quebec's Railway Bridge is painted green, whereas the Forth Railway Bridge is red! We then drove on to see a famous Catholic Church due east of Quebec City. On the way, we stopped off at Montmorency Falls on the Montmorency River, which plummet 276 feet into the St. Lawrence River. They were absolutely beautiful and had a silky look about them.

There were a number of windsurfers nearby, speeding along the St. Lawrence River. Our next stop was to visit the Basilica of St. Anne de Beaupre, a church made of silver granite which is 300ft high to the foot of the steeple crosses. We walked around the church where there were may attractive mosaics and a beautiful statue representing St. Anne holding the child Mary in her right arm. St. Anne is wearing a crown because she was officially proclaimed Patroness of Quebec. At the statue it is said miraculous healings have taken place. The exterior of the church was very impressive and we heard the bells ringing – a wonderful sound.

Later we drove on to our hotel, the Chateau Frontenac; it was very elegant. The reception area had beautiful wooden panelling with paintings and the lifts had brass doors inscribed with the emblems of every State in Canada. Our room too was very attractive with white doors with brass fittings. After unloading our gear in the room we walked up St. Louis Street, which was very quaint with lots of character and atmosphere and then on, under the beautiful St. Louis Gate, and into Grande Allée. We saw a few horse-drawn carriages plodding up the street and observed the Parliament buildings, the seat of the National Assembly. As we walked up Grande Allée, a superb tree-lined avenue with lots of attractive homes lining it and many restaurants, we saw a statue of the French General Montcalm. Our meal was at a French restaurant, where I had a delicious lobster dish.

We walked into Battlefield Park close by which is a 235-acre site, also known as the Plains of Abraham. A battle commenced here on 13th September 1759 between the British and French armies, the French led by the Marquis de Montcalm and the British by General Wolfe. The battle was won by the British. Ironically, both generals later died as a result of their war injuries. We walked on alongside the Quebec Citadel which is the largest fortification in North America and is still garrisoned by regular troops of the Royal 22nd Regiment. We saw many cannons scattered around.

We walked to the headland of Cap Daimant overlooking the St. Lawrence River and had fabulous views of yachts and speed boats skimming across the water. We looked across the river to the town of Levis, named after the French general Levis who tried unsuccessfully to recapture Quebec City from the English in 1760. The British victory was affirmed by the Treaty of Paris in 1763. We walked down St. Louis Street again and saw a cannon ball embedded in the base of a tree, no doubt a relic from the battle in 1759. We passed the Place d'Armes with its lovely Neo-Gothic fountain; behind this is Rue d'Tresor, which is known as "Artists Lane." It was here we purchased some etchings of Quebec City. Then, upon arriving back at our hotel, the Chateau Frontenac, we strolled onto the massive wooden terrace at the front, called Terrasse Dufferin. There was also a statue here of Samuel de Champlain, who arrived here in 1608. He founded the colony of Place Royale and Petite Champlain, the oldest part of the city, which we could see below from our vantage point on the terrace. The name Quebec is derived from the Indian word *kebec*, meaning, "where the river narrows". UNESCO has proclaimed Quebec City a World Heritage treasure.

The following day we travelled to Ottawa, whose history traces back to Champlain's voyage of 1613, and drove along the shoreline of the St. Lawrence for quite some miles. Many houses had a lot of style, and there were many typical Canadian red-roofed farmsteads. We came through a place called Trois Rivières (where three rivers meet), which is one of the oldest settlements in Canada, dating back 1634, where we saw a beautiful Gothic church. We travelled into the nation's capital, Ottawa, over the McDonald Cartier Bridge and drove to the Governor General's residence at Rideau Hall to see the changing of the guard to the sound of bagpipes. We also saw the large stately mansions which were diplomats' houses. We stayed at the Four Seasons Hotel for one night. Later we walked to the parliament buildings on Parliament Hill, the highest point for miles around and the site chosen for the seat of the Canadian Government by Queen Victoria in 1857.

The buildings are distinctive by their green copper roofs and Neo-Gothic architecture. The beautiful Peace Tower is the focal point, towering 291ft, and housing the 53 carillon bells, whose beautifully resounding peals can be heard across the town. When there is a light shining on the top of the Peace Tower it means Parliament is sitting. The Eternal Flame at the front of the parliament buildings commemorates Canada's 1967 centennial of nationhood. Ottawa River runs behind the parliament buildings.

We passed the Chateau Laurier Hotel nearby, owned by the Canadian Pacific Railway Company – an attractive building with conical roofs.

We strolled around the Byward Market to see on display the cornucopia of lovely fruit, flowers vegetables and sea food. There was a great atmosphere here with a brass band playing. We later observed Canada's biggest treasure, the Royal Mint. On the walk back to our hotel we saw a few cruisers coming up through the locks on the Rideau Canal. Close by is a beautiful war memorial commemorating the First and Second World Wars and the Korean War respectively.

We travelled from Ottawa to Toronto and stopped off at 1,000 Islands on the St. Lawrence River. We drove onto Hill Island over the 1,000 Islands Peace Bridge which links American and Canadian borders. On Hill Island we ascended the 400ft. Skydeck Tower, for a panoramic vista of the beautiful, tree-covered islands for a distance of 25 miles. It was from here we observed the paddle steamer *Alexandra Belle* in the distance. There are numerous beautiful and expensive holiday homes on the islands, and naturally, everyone needs the use of a boat for commuting to and from the mainland, so jetties and boathouses are commonplace. From the 1,000 Islands we drove towards Toronto passing Oshawa, one of the main centres of the Canadian automobile industry. As we approached Toronto the roads merged into many lanes, probably six in either direction, and were very busy.

We drove down River Valley Parkway passing Fort York which was established in 1793. Retreating British soldiers blew it up in 1813, throwing the American forces into confusion and killing most of them. We observed a naval destroyer *H.M.C.S. Haida* and huge marina. We also had a good view of three manmade islands called Ontario Place, another Expo site with a space-like spherical geodesic dome. Later, we visited High Park, a beautiful parkland. There was a fantastic arbour with very colourful hanging baskets, a perfect show of flowers. In front of a lake there was also a floral display depicting a large Maple Leaf. We spotted numerous black squirrels here. Finally we drove on to our hotel, the Four Seasons Inn On The Park, which was pleasantly situated amongst lush, expansive parkland. The hotel had good facilities with a spacious bedroom and bathroom which made it easier for me. Exploring the hotel complex, we saw a pond with huge koi carp swimming around and an attractive bridge. The complex itself was set in very pleasant grounds with beautiful trees, flower beds and a large swimming pool.

We had dinner in the C.N. Towers revolving restaurant at 1,150ft high, but the overall height of the tower is 1,815ft – making it the tallest free-standing building in the world. We had some difficulty getting into the tower – Dad had to bump me down a flight of stairs, then down an escalator only just wide enough for the wheelchair. At the foot of the tower there is a new building called the Skydome, a large sports complex with a retractable roof, which had just recently been opened. From the restaurant we had spectacular views over the city of Toronto including the Toronto Islands with their vast parklands and marinas and other city landmarks.

The next day, after a leisurely breakfast in the hotel, we journeyed to downtown Toronto, parked the hired car then started to walk up Bay Street, known as the Wall Street of Canada and second only to New York's Wall Street. We passed the Old City Hall, a rather elegant building, Next door is the New City Hall, which has twin curved buildings completed in 1965. Immediately in front of the building is a large pool which, in the winter, freezes over and people skate on it. We walked to the attractive pink sandstone Provincial Parliament Building in Queens Park. Then we wandered around the large shopping centre called the Eaton Centre. The exterior of the building was rather like an enormous glass conservatory. It was here that we chatted to a Canadian lady in a café called Pumpkinheads. In the course of our conversation, she suggested we visited the Scarborough Bluffs, overlooking, the massive Lake Ontario, so off we set and visited Bluffers Park to have a good view of Scarborough Bluffs. Here, I observed a colony of over two hundred Canada geese, beautiful birds! There was also a large marina. We had afternoon tea at the Guild Country Inn set in a park with art and historic treasures, overlooking the majestic view of Lake Ontario from the Scarborough Bluffs. The Guild Inn was opened in 1932, and houses works of art by famous Canadian artists. I observed a few Canadian robins in the grounds. It was an interesting place to visit.

The following day we journeyed to Niagara Falls; on the way we saw the lovely tree-carpeted Niagara escarpment and passed many orchards. We drove over the Welland Canal, a 26-mile man-made wonder that links Lake Ontario to Lake Erie, and saw one of the huge lift locks. We stopped off at the town of Niagara-on-the-Lake, which is located at the Northern end of the 35-mile-long Niagara Parkway and enjoyed a leisurely breakfast at the Moffatt Inn while sitting in the conservatory part of the hotel. In the mid 1830s Niagara-on-the-Lake was a prosperous town with fine houses and a growing shipbuilding industry. Said to be one of the prettiest towns in North America, it had beautifully restored buildings. It was here we walked into a fudge-making shop to see how the fudge was made on an old marble slab and all the processes involved. We sampled some fudge which was simply delicious and considered good enough to take with us!

Next stop-off was Fort George which was built in the 1790s. There were massive ramparts here and large cannons to see. We motored down Niagara Parkway where you can see many splendid houses. The Niagara River was a beautiful blue. We came through Queenston, an historical town on the Niagara Parkway where we saw the Brock Monument, named after General Isaac Brock, a Canadian hero in the war of 1812. He died leading the troops to victory over the American forces in the battle of Queenston Heights. We also saw the Niagara floral clock made up of 25,000 flowers and the world's largest floral clock. There were many parks in this area with lovely manicured lawns, fabulous trees and flowers in full bloom.

Our next stop was the Niagara River Gorge Walk Adventure. Here we went in a lift down to river level and then walked on an elevated walkway to the edge of Whirlpool Rapids. The river was moving with mighty power, crashing and banging against the rocks with amazing force. It was an exhilarating feeling watching the river flow. Incidentally, it was here in 1883 that Captain Matthew Webb tried to challenge the river's power by seeing if he could swim across its turbulent waters. Sadly, he drowned in Whirlpool Rapids and his body was found a few days later at Queenston.

Other dare-devils have challenged Niagara's might by doing such stunts as going over the falls in a barrel. The first person to do this successfully was a female teacher, no less! This practice was eventually outlawed.

A short time later we had our first glimpse of the spectacular Niagara Falls, God's workmanship in all its splendour. We continued driving down the Niagara Parkway to Fort Erie, on the shore of Lake Erie, seeing some lovely mansions which had character and most of which had their own private boat launches. At Fort Erie we walked around the fort which saw active duty in the war of 1812. As we explored the fort a young man was dressed in period uniform as a sentry. We saw all the cannons placed in strategic positions. They had military displays each day when local school children dressed up in period uniform to re-enact battle scenes when cannons were fired. We then drove back to the Canadian side of Niagara Falls and went down Table Rock Scenic Tunnels for a most dramatic view of the Horseshoe Falls on the Canadian side and the American Falls. We had to wear yellow plastic capes to protect ourselves from the spray. The falls are absolutely incredible, and your eyes widen in awe: a really spectacular sight and the din is quite deafening. Close by, the Canadian Falls plunge 176ft down and are very wide. We watched the famous boat, *The Maid of the Mist,* sail very close to the falls and then abruptly make an about turn. We also gained an excellent view of the American Falls which are a 1,000ft wide and plunge 182ft. There were some very impressive rainbows.

The two waterfalls send 2,831,000 litres of water per second thundering into the Niagara River – which is staggering. Not surprisingly, a proportion of Niagara's water is always used to generate electricity. The actual flow of water cascading over the falls is 50% during the day and 75% at night; this is achieved by adjusting huge sluice gates which control the river's flow.

We then drove to our hotel which was on the American side of the falls, crossing over Rainbow Bridge, a very apt name. We travelled onto Goat Island between the American falls and the Canadian Horseshoe Falls. It was a lovely island with numerous trees and parkland.

In the evening we had a very pleasant meal in the Minolta Towers Rainbow Room. The tower is 400ft tall and we were lucky to have a table with a view overlooking the falls. It was fascinating watching the sun setting, creating lovely scenes of light combining with the spray of the falls. Later the falls were attractively illuminated with alternating pink, green and white light. We had arrived at the restaurant at 6.30pm and left at 10.30pm, such was the spectacle!

Next day we travelled to Ithaca in the Finger Lakes region of New York State. It was a rather complicated drive out of Niagara as there are so many roads. The Finger Lakes region of UpState New York is so called because it resembles fingers on the map. It is a land of lakes, waterfalls, steep gorges, wooded glens and vineyards – there are 25 wineries.

We drove through a town called Canandaigua, which is a Seneca Indian word meaning "chosen place" and has beautiful churches and many attractive houses. There is a pretty lake here also called Canandaigua. It was here we observed some ducks, including mallards. Then we drove down to Seneca Lake which is 40 miles long and 640ft deep, making it the deepest lake east of the Rockies. We did a short detour to Keuka Lake and had a picnic lunch overlooking it. It was beautiful scenery. While picnicking in the glorious sunshine we observed a sea plane taking off from the lake.

Later we stopped off at Watkins Glen State Park, at the southern end of Seneca Lake. There is a two-mile gorge walk here. We saw a tunnel at the foot of the gorge walk and the very high gorge walls. We drove to the south entrance of Watkins Glen where a park policeman in a patrol car very kindly escorted us down a service road to a bridge which spanned the gorgeous gorge. This was a steep and winding road with beautiful trees, past a lovely lily pond. From the bridge we had a good view of the gorge, and saw a few waterfalls and raging rapids. In one part of the gorge a large fallen tree was wedged across and the water was cascading over it.

The rock layers of the gorge walls were formed from sediments which accumulated under water 370 million years ago – simply mind blowing!

We then travelled along the eastern side of Seneca for a short distance, passing Hector Falls which were absolutely beautiful; the water cascaded over rocky steps in what looked like strands of lace. A detour, due to roadworks, took us through a lot of farmland. Looking back, we had fantastic vistas of Seneca Lake. Near Trumansburg we stopped in a State Park to see Taughannock Falls, 215ft high, and plunging into a huge rock amphitheatre. The guide books say that they are the highest waterfalls east of the American Rockies. Having had a good view of the waterfalls we drove on to our hotel in Ithaca.

After settling in we strolled into downtown Ithaca, passing the City Hall, and looked around Ithaca Commons, a small shopping area which has been pedestrianised since 1976. The buildings here have been restored to their former glory, and we spent some time exploring them. The pedestrian area was ideal for negotiating the wheelchair with its flat smooth pavements. After an evening meal we travelled a short distance south to a place called Newfield, to see an historic covered bridge which was built in 1852. There was a lovely hillside flanking us and fabulous sunlight at this time of the evening. We stopped off at Buttermilk Falls, a wonderful sight, you could swim right out to the foot of the falls. The sunlight on the falls looked very attractive. Later that evening we travelled on to Stewart Park on the shore of Cayuga Lake which is 38 miles long – an attractive parkland with a fabulous duck pond and many trees. We observed a lighthouse in the harbour area and noted that the U.S. lighthouse service marked its 200th anniversary that year, 1989.

Our last full day was spent motoring back to New York, travelling through a lot of farmland and beautiful rolling wooded hillsides. After being on the road a couple of hours, we stopped off at Binghampton for a leisurely breakfast at Denny's restaurant, a well-known chain in America. After breakfast we came through more hilly and mountainous terrain with beautiful crystal-clear rivers running through the valleys. Then suddenly, I saw a massive bird which I recognised as being a golden eagle soaring above us. This monarch of the sky was surveying the area in search of food, I expect. We travelled on through a small village called Colchester, then through the southern portion of the Catskill Mountains 50 miles north of New York City. A very short time later we drove into Harriman Mountain State Park and Bear Mountain State Park, very pleasant areas with attractive lakes. We motored to the top of Bear Mountain, elevation 1350ft, and from the top we had a panoramic vista of the Hudson River, rocky outcrops and a vast carpet of innumerable trees stretching out to the horizon.

Next stop-off was Bear Mountain Lodge for lunch – a fabulous log cabin-style building which fitted in well with its surroundings. There was a policeman on horseback outside the lodge and also a military helicopter from the famous West Point Military Academy, which is on the banks of the Hudson River. We ate our lunch outside, with the beautiful warm sunshine beating down on us. I had a huge salad sandwich which was delicious. There was a beautiful lake near Bear Lodge with lovely trees surrounding it.

We drove south of Bear Mountain onto the Palisades InterState Parkway into New York City over the George Washington Bridge. It was opened in 1931, with six lanes on the lower deck and eight lanes on top! From the bridge we could see the Manhattan skyline including the Chrysler Building and the Empire State Building. As we came off the bridge the highway branched out into twelve lanes and it was extremely busy. We passed Flushing Meadows parkland and sports complex where the famous tennis tournaments are held.

We stayed overnight at the J.F.K. Hilton Hotel. From the hotel room window we could see brilliant sunsets over New York City and also watch numerous types of aircraft coming in to land, many of them huge 747s.

The following day I was very fortunate to fly home again on Concorde and it was a first for Mum! We arrived at the airport at 7.10am and after going through all the formalities, we proceeded to British Airways Concorde lounge where we had a Bucks Fizz, croissants and pastries for breakfast. There was an excellent view of Concorde from the lounge. We then boarded the plane, and I sat on the third row this time. We had to wait for 15 minutes on the runway, as there was a queue of eight planes in front of us waiting to take off. Then came the time for us to take off, too – a loud roar, the brake off and *blast off*, it was all systems go.

We took off at 250mph then Concorde gradually speeded up to Mach 2, twice the speed of sound. A few minutes after take-off we saw Long Island Sound. Once again, I kept a close eye on those computer dials in front of us: our height went up to 57,000ft, and the maximum speed was up to 1390mph, which is truly amazing. We could see the curvature of the earth slightly. I had a superb meal, starting off with mouth-watering caviar and prawn canapés. For the main course I chose lightly curried Maine lobster, cheese and biscuits followed by a glass of port. We had a very fast landing – it was an exhilarating feeling following a sensational flight of three hours and 22 minutes flying time. We then had to rush to get the last shuttle back to Manchester but we made it! The Concorde flight was a special end to a memorable holiday.

Chapter 18

Birds, Birds, Birds and More Birds....

I have become enthusiastic about birds – strictly the feathered kind of course! This is a pastime that I can readily get involved with. My parents and I frequently travel to birding spots with the aid of RSPB (Royal Society for the Protection of Birds) and WWT (Wildfowl and Wetlands Trust) booklets and other general knowledge gained from friends and the Internet. Apart from watching any birds in their natural habitat I also get excited at the prospect of new sightings, particularly rarities. However, I stress I am not a "twitcher".

My interest began after some experimental efforts made painting stones at the age of 13. I started with images such as the cartoon character "Snoopy" and simple patterns. Later on, aged 16, this interest developed into painting birds on stones and slates, with occasional commissions from friends. I remember when I was a young teen my parents and I would go down to the beach picking up stones and pebbles of the right size and shape. My interest in birds developed from these early years.

Although I used to go out with my parents looking at different birds, watching their antics and enjoying every moment, it was not until 1990 when I joined the RSPB that my interest really took off.

I thought it would be helpful if I told you that, even in a wheelchair and frequently on a ventilator, I have managed to visit many bird sites in the UK. I have travelled to more than 50 sites – some are RSPB reserves, others are run by the WWT (which I joined as a member in 1998), local councils and naturalist groups such as the Deeside Naturalist Society near to my home in Chester, where I can readily use the family car as a hide.

My favourite birding locations obviously have to be linked to my disability in that they have easy access for my parents to help me on my adventures. I would like to summarise what I believe to be my top ten bird sites from the point of interest, ease of accessibility and bird varieties:

MINSMERE – This site is the RSPB's flagship reserve. A special permit can be obtained on the day to allow disabled people to drive their cars right up to the hides, which we did. When I first got out of the car and into the wheelchair someone could be heard bellowing, "There is a Little Egret nearby". A moment later to my amazement the egret flew low over the car. This was my first sighting of this lovely bird. A speciality bird at Minsmere is the Avocet – a wader. With its upturned bill and black and white plumage, the Avocet is an elegant bird.

LEIGHTON MOSS – Situated in Lancashire between Carnforth and Silverdale, Leighton Moss reserve comprises massive reed beds, lagoons and woodland areas. Speciality birds are the Bittern, the Marsh Harrier and the Water Rail. There is good wheelchair access to the several hides around the reserve which are linked by gravel paths – a bit bumpy but OK. I have been in most of the hides, but my favourite is probably less than 100 metres from the car park. It is called the "Lillian Hide" and situated in its centre front is a huge picture window giving wonderful views across the reed beds and open lake. From here I have observed Marsh Harriers flying around and displaying. A new addition to this hide is a hearing "loop" to enable the hard of hearing to listen to audio and taped commentaries. I have been fortunate in seeing the elusive Bittern on two occasions and heard the male "booming" on another. The first sighting stands out in my memory, for the bird's plumage was clearly visible as it flew a fair distance to its nesting area. There were a number of other people in the hide at the time who clapped and cheered when they saw this shy and secretive bird. A rare delight!

MARTIN MERE – This is a Wildfowl and Wetlands Trust reserve located close to Ormskirk in Lancashire. There are captive birds here from all over the world. Interesting though they are, and it is good to check up on them, my primary interests are the wild bird areas serviced by many hides. Most of them are accessible by wheelchair

The reserve has good tarmac paths and an excellent large glass-windowed observatory. There is a large gated entrance close to this observatory, normally kept closed but kindly opened for me on request by a phone call prior to our arrival. This makes it possible to drive a car up alongside the hide, which is quite helpful on cold days, with equipment to carry – in our case the ventilator plus the birding paraphernalia. From this heated observatory it is ideal to watch the wintering Whooper Swans and Bewick Swans. On one occasion, to my amazement, a Spoonbill appeared close by with its large spoon shaped bill. It was good watching its feeding action, making broad sweeps from side to side with its bill; probably ten minutes or so later it flew off, ghost-like into the air. Superb!

DUNGENESS – This area is on the South-Eastern tip of Britain. It is renowned as having the best example of cuspate shingle foreland in Europe and was the RSPB's first reserve, set up in 1931. It comprises a group of gravel pits, the main one being Burrowes Pit. A permit may be obtained to drive up to some hides to make it easier for wheelchair access. Shingle is a pain to be pushed on! The hides give clear visibility over the main pit. It was here I spotted my first Ringed Plover. A good visitors' centre also overlooks Burrowes Pit with large picture windows. It was from here I also saw my first Grey Plover and Arctic Terns. As we were driving out of the reserve, still on my first visit, I spotted another first – a female Hobby showing off its aerial displays.

Another highlight worth a mention is spotting my first female smews on a windswept February afternoon. I had an excellent view of the birds. They are members of the Saw Bill family of duck.

LLANELLI – This is the only Wildfowl and Wetlands Trust reserve in Wales housing captive birds in pens. The reserve has been extended to encompass a 200-acre water park as a refuge for wild birds, called the Millennium Wetlands. In this new area we walked into a very impressive hide called the Heron Wing observatory. From the outside it resembles a stylised heron elevated on a bank with slanted glass panels inclined at 45 degrees reaching to the floor, giving a sweeping panorama of the new development. Amongst the birds seen from here were Little Egrets, Heron, Godwits and Little Grebe. If you are fortunate enough it is possible to see five species of British owls – Barn Owl, Tawny Owl, Little Owl, Short-eared Owl and Long-eared Owl. I didn't see them but hope to next time! However, I did see a new bird here which was great, it was the Spotted Redshank.

SLIMBRIDGE – Another Wildfowl and Wetlands Trust reserve and the headquarters for the Trust. The WWT was founded in 1946 by Sir Peter Scott, who also lived here. I have visited this reserve on a number of occasions, again there are captive bred birds as well as birds in the wild. Good tarmac paths and a number of accessible hides for wheelchairs are features to be found on this site. In the year 2000 a fantastic redevelopment opened providing better facilities for both visitors and staff alike. It includes a lecture theatre and the Sloane Tower, providing a brilliant panorama of the whole site from an elevated position. The tower is equipped with a lift for wheelchairs. Also in the visitors centre are an art gallery and exhibition areas with interactive educational opportunities for children. I have had some really good bird watching opportunities on this site. One good birding experience here at Slimbridge was while watching a large flock of Teal, mainly female, at quite close range. Suddenly the Teal panicked and took to flight, and I remember commenting at the time to Mum and Dad, "There must be a bird of prey around." I scanned the skies and lo and behold there were two Buzzards wheeling around in search of a tasty snack.

CAERLAVEROCK – A Wildfowl and Wetlands Trust reserve on the Solway Firth on the West coast of Scotland. I have been to this reserve once to date. We had come here to see the thousands of wintering Barnacle Geese which fly in from the Island of Spitzbergen in the Arctic circle. We were given permission to drive outside most of the hides which was really handy, avoiding a long walk and the risk of breathing in too much cold air via the ventilator. At this reserve I spotted 7,150 Barnacle Geese, the first time that I had seen this species of geese in the wild. Another first was seeing Yellow Hammers which was great. I came back to this reserve later on that day for a badger watch. This was held in part of a farm building which is converted mainly for B&B accommodation and incorporates a sun lounge overlooking the main lake and the snow-capped Skiddaw mountain, which looked majestic with its Alpen glow. In the sun lounge, a platform was improvised to elevate me a foot or so in order to give me greater visibility. After waiting about an hour and a half a badger came onto the stage immediately in front of the building, then another and another until in the end we had four all attracted by honey which had been daubed onto logs in front of our window. The build-up prior to the badger watch included sightings of various birds including a group of Whooper Swans and more Barnacles with an interesting commentary, with questions, given by a warden. Also that evening I had a short glimpse of a Barn Owl. It was a very peaceful and tranquil time on a crisp, clear star studded night – a fitting end to the day.

CONWAY – An RSPB reserve which is a 45-minute drive from my home in Chester. It was opened in 1995 and land-scaped using much of the spoil from the construction of the Conway Tunnel. I have visited this reserve many times and it has been interesting to see it grow and develop over the years. The visitor centre has large picture windows and a shop, is a stone's throw from the car park, and affords good views of the reserve, the Conway River valley and the castle. Most of the hides are wheelchair-friendly, served by good gravel paths and a board walk. I have had some good bird watching forays here. On one particular visit I was fortunate to spot my first and only elusive Water Rail.

BARN ELMS – Barn Elms is the latest Wildfowl and Wetlands Trust reserve. Known as the Wetland Centre, it is sit-uated close to the centre of London, a short distance from Hammersmith Bridge. The reserve fulfilled the lifetime dream of WWT founder, the late Sir Peter Scott, to build a bird reserve in central London. There are wild and captive birds here, and good facilities for disabled and wheelchair users. Hides are readily accessible, one in particular, the Peacock Tower, pos-sesses a lift giving excellent views of the reserve. The paths are good, mainly tarmac which is an ideal surface for wheelchair occupants and their pushers. In the visitor centre complex is a fantastic observatory with huge plate glass windows extending upwards to all floors. In appearance, the building resembles an aircraft terminal giving a wonderful view over the main lake. Of my three visits to Barn Elms the main highlights have been watching the courtship-flying displays of the the Little Ringed Plover as they seek to attract a mate by showing off their flying prowess. Another highlight was seeing a large group of male and female Gadwall Ducks at very close range.

RUTLAND WATER – There are two Wildlife Trust Reserves here, Lyndon and Egleton, both situated near Oakham, in Rutland. I have visited the Egleton reserve on a few occasions. My first trip in 1996 was at the start of the Osprey Project. This is a five-year project during which translocated Osprey chicks, taken from Scotland, are transported to Rutland Water. Upon arrival the young Ospreys are kept in huge holding pens and are fed by a surrogate human 'mother'. This begins around July and by September the young Ospreys are ready to leave for Africa to return, hopefully, to Rutland Water two years later to breed. The whole movement is being monitored by attaching radio transmitters to the birds and tracked by satellite. On this first trip I was fortunate to spot the four translocated Ospreys, which was fantastic!

The hides are accessible to wheelchairs, and there is an excellent visitors' centre which is now extended to cater for visitors and schools alike. Permission can be obtained for wheelchairs to park outside the centre which overlooks the main lagoon, giving wide sweeping views from the large picture windows.

The year 2001 marked the end of the five-year Osprey translocation project and the achievement of its major goal when, for the first time in central England for 150 years, one of the Ospreys from the project bred. Shortly after this event I visited Rutland Water's Egleton reserve for a weekend. One day I was lucky enough to spot six Ospreys, including one that took to the air. The following day I spotted the male Osprey tagged '09' on its large nest perched high in a tree, and suddenly five Ospreys were seen in flight. What an impressive sight it was watching them soar above Lax Hill! Two other delights of my visits to this reserve were when I observed an Egyptian Goose and Tree Sparrows for the first time. It's a good place to see Tree Sparrows.

SPINNIES – A nature reserve on the North Wales Coast, near Bangor. It has two hides, one accessible to wheelchairs. One side of this hide overlooks the Aber Ogwen Estuary and the other a small lake with reed beds. The inside of this hide has good visibility through shuttered openings. There are good tarmaced paths leading from the car park. The birds that I have spotted on my visits here are a Kingfisher (a flash of turquoise darting low over the water), Greenshank by the lake area, Red Breasted Mergansers, Mute Swans, Shelduck, hundreds of Oystercatchers and Greylag Geese, to name the main sightings.

RYE MEADS MARSH (formerly Rye House Marsh) – A North London RSPB reserve comprised of reed beds, open water, meadows and a nature trail, which is accessible to wheelchairs. The trail path is mainly firm gravel, apart from a section of boardwalk. I have been in two of the five hides accessible to wheelchairs, one of which overlooks a small tree-enclosed lake renowned for attracting Kingfishers to an artificial nesting bank. On my first visit I was fortunate to see a Kingfisher, but it was on my second visit that I watched two Kingfishers putting on a real show for some time, diving for minnows and returning to their perch, a branch overhanging the water's edge. In addition to diving, I watched the Kingfishers flying over the lake, a beautiful sight, certainly a highlight of any visit to the reserve. But, to our surprise and amazement as we walked back to the car, an Osprey on migration back to Africa flew low over the reserve after plucking a young crow from its nest, causing quite a commotion for the startled crows!

WELNEY – A Wildfowl and Wetlands Trust reserve, located in the Fenlands of Cambridgeshire, where there are solely and wholly wild birds. You park the car on one side of the road in the visitor centre car park and cross the road into the reserve via a large concrete ramp and go over a bridge which traverses a main drainage dyke. Immediately in front of you as you come off the bridge is a huge heated observatory giving a grand panorama of the reserve. In the winter this observatory is a brilliant and warm place to watch the thousands of visiting Whooper and Bewick Swans, plus thousands of male Pochards with a small number of females. The reserve is flooded in the winter for the influx of wildfowl and drained, to a certain level to attract waders such as the Avocet, in the summer. I have only visited one of the hides, this came about when returning to the car park I read on the recent sightings board in the visitor centre, 'Red Necked Phalarope'. The sighting was also confirmed by the person on the admissions desk, who said that a fellow birder had seen the bird earlier that afternoon. This aroused the "twitcher" in me so much so that instead of driving off as planned, we did a U-turn and chased off in pursuit of this bird. Once in the hide, full of nervous anticipation, we scanned the body of water in front of us with binoculars and there it was – the Red Necked Phalarope busily feeding using its unique spinning action as it went. A mega tick. (Twitcher terminology!!) Another experience was seeing a Barn Owl, to my amazement, at 2.30pm on a winter's afternoon. It first flew onto a post giving a fantastic view of its ghostly plumage, then flew off, then we reversed the car and saw it again flying a few hundred yards.

BLACKTOFT SANDS – An RSPB reserve near Goole in the East Riding of Yorkshire. The reserve comprises a tidal reed marsh, reed beds, brackish lagoons and salt marsh. We were allowed to park outside the reception hide which was useful. Once inside the hide, which is split into two levels with a ramp, there are excellent large picture windows overlooking the expansive reed beds. From here I spotted Avocets flying low along the tidal water channel. From the reception hide we strolled a short distance to Xerox Hide; from here I observed the Avocets again plus my first sightings of Dunlin and Ruff which were clothed in their summer plumage. Whilst I was watching these birds a large fox came prowling around. On my other visits to this reserve I came in the winter to try and see wintering Hen Harriers and was fortunate to watch a female Hen Harrier, known as a Ringtail, sailing across the reed beds – brilliant!

MARSHSIDE – Another RSPB reserve near Southport in Lancashire and part of the internationally important Ribble estuary. Marshside possesses some of the best lowland wet grassland in the north-west of England. The reserve can be seen from the roads which pass by it. There are two main approach roads and I have managed to see many birds without leaving the car, such as wintering Wigeon in their thousands, Shoveler Ducks and thousands of Lapwings – to name a few. There are two good hides, the main one is wheelchair-accessible and doubles up as a small office with display boards. It is possible to park close to the hide in the car park, but we park in front of the sand re-cycling factory over the road. It is easier and provides a little bit of protection from the cold. The hide itself has excellent visibility and is a good height for the wheelchair. Amongst the birds I have seen from here are Golden Plover, Lapwing, Shoveler, Bar-tailed and Black-tailed Godwits, the Merlin bird of prey, Kestrel and Teal. My first visit coincided with a big high tide and as we were driving back on Southport's coastal road there were literally thousands upon thousands of various types of Gull overhead and floating on the sea. It made Alfred Hitchcock's film, *The Birds* seem tame in comparison! What a spectacle to end my first visit to Marshside.

Other sites worthy of mention and of interest are:
Connah's Quay in Flintshire, by the Powergen Power Station on the Dee Estuary. This site is on my local patch and is run by the Deeside Naturalist Society of which I am a member. Although I have been in one of the hides here, we more often than not use the car as a hide. A good tarmac road surrounds the site. I have had some memorable bird spottings on this estuarine site.

Pennington Flash Country Park, near Leigh in Lancashire. It is a reliable place to see the elusive Long-eared Owl, particularly in the winter. We went in November 1999 to try and see the owl but it did not appear on this occasion and we returned home. A few days later we rang the warden on the site to ask about the owls and he volunteered to ring us back when they were likely to be seen. A week later he telephoned to say that the Long-eared Owls had been seen earlier that morning. So off we

My painting of a Long-eared Owl

155

went and the warden met us on arrival and escorted us to the place where he had seen the owl. It took me a while to focus on the bird, but with the help of a sketch by the warden to show its location, Eureka! It was so well camouflaged against the tree it was perched in. Its posture was elongated with its ear tufts erect: this is an attitude which the owl adopts when it is wary, probably sensing our presence. Top marks for this warden's help and skills.

Loch Garten RSPB Reserve in Speyside, 10 miles East of Aviemore, which is famous for breeding Ospreys. The visitor centre hide overlooks the Ospreys' eyrie. There is also CCTV camera on the nest relaying live pictures back to the visitor centre.

Another site worth a visit is **Gigrin Farm**, a Red Kite feeding station in mid-Wales, just south of Rhayader. (See the piece on Gigrin Farm below).

A final recommended site is a nature reserve just south of **Welshpool**. This has an artificial bank specially designed for Sand Martins. There is only one hide here, but it is an excellent one set on stilts and only a short walk from the car park on gravel paths.

Drawing on my bird-watching experiences on bird reserves I have noticed that the viewing slats in the hides on some reserves are either too low or too high and feel the solution to this problem is to have viewing slats at different levels to cater for differing eye levels, particularly for wheelchair users. Similarly, the path surfaces, inclines and hide interiors should be kept at the forefront of the designers' minds when seeking to make improvements so that the reserves are more friendly for all visitors including wheelchair users.

I wrote the following two accounts after particularly memorable birding experiences:

A TRIP TO GIGRIN FARM KITE FEEDING STATION.

It was a cloudy start to our journey but as we approached Rhayader the sun began to shine on the snow-laden Welsh mountainside. Nearer the place now! We parked the car alongside a hide with good wheelchair access, and which was situated overlooking the field which was to be observed. Just before 2.00pm the farmer appeared scattering offal obtained from the local butcher. The offal was used to attract the Kites, but not before an important prelude had been played: the appearance of Ravens, Carrion Crows and Magpies before the grand entrance of the majestic *Milvus milvus* alias the Red Kite. Incidentally, the Kites would not feed until the Ravens and their consorts had sampled the food.

The Kites put on quite a show, swooping and gliding to display their acrobatic prowess as they descended to gather the morsels of carrion from the ground. It was the sun which revealed the full glory of the Kites' chestnut brown and grey plumage. We must have watched for 45 minutes or more, then suddenly, without warning, a Buzzard swept across our line of vision. It landed and began feeding to the apparent dismay of the Ravens, which immediately began mobbing the intruder, who nonchalantly carried on eating its fill. The Buzzard provided a fitting end to an enjoyable day at Gigrin Farm.

FINDING MY HOLY GRAIL AT RYE MARSH RESERVE

It was a beautiful sunny day in August and we were on our way to a wedding in Essex. I had read previously of the RSPB reserve at Rye House Marsh near to our wedding venue at Brentford. The wedding over, the following day we were looking out for the reserve near Junction 25 on the M25. It was extremely hot when we arrived at the reserve's car park. We unloaded my wheelchair and made our way to a small lake with a man-made bank where we hoped to see a Kingfisher, a hope I had carried for many years. As we walked, for a mile or so, we passed an expanse of reed beds, heard the chattering of a Reed Warbler and on the River Lee, which ran to our left, saw a flotilla of Canada Geese.

A two-story hide made viewing possible at the lake. We watched the bank and surrounding area for half an hour or so before a return to the car was necessary for a "refresher" on my ventilator. The rest of the group watched on while I was refreshed. Some refreshment! The group returned 10 minutes later with the news, "We have seen a Kingfisher!" As my time of refreshment continued and everyone waited, a warden passed by and offered us the use of a second wheelchair on which to carry my ventilator and battery pack. What an excellent offer – for it enabled me to venture out for longer periods, so increasing my chances of seeing the elusive Kingfisher.

I couldn't wait to get back to the lakeside hide. Suddenly, lo and behold, a Kingfisher appeared, alighting on a post some three metres in front of our position. The bird's plumage appeared like a glittering jewel, iridescent in the sunlight and arrayed in magnificence of colour, turquoise, green and orange. It was an exciting moment: the Kingfisher pivoted around to reveal its front view before darting off into the trees. It was a hard act to follow, albeit a momentary one. Some Coots tried hard as they chased one another across the lake and we did glimpse a Common Tern as we made our way back to the cars, but the Kingfisher graced the show and will remain indelibly marked in my memory at the end of another perfect day.

Chapter 19

Ventilation

In September 1989 it was thought the use of a ventilator would help whilst I was sleeping because my breathing goes shallower during the REM period of sleep (see page 173). I wasn't very happy about using it to start with because it was foreign to me but very slowly got used to it.

In April 1990 when we went to London for a short break, we took Grandma and Grandad with us. On the morning of the second day I had a bit of phlegm and before it had cleared we set out from Dad's company flat and walked towards Harrods store. We, that is, Grandma, Mum and myself waited while Dad and Grandad went off to find a chemist's shop to purchase a bottle of expectorant, a liquid solution which helps disperse "muck" i.e. phlegm from the throat. A momentary breeze took my breath away whilst we waited for Dad to return and despite taking a sip of the expectorant, it was decided to seek warmer and stiller air conditions inside. We moved inside the Harrods Store but the phlegm became a problem which caused me to choke in an effort to secure free passage for air. It was at this point Dad decided to take me back to the flat. Apparently on the way back I lost consciousness. I can recall reaching the threshold of the flat complex and seeing a man just about to come out of the building ... the rest is a blur. Dad told me later that this man helped him to get me into the lift and into the flat when time was critical. Dad also told me that this man advised on the technique of artificial respiration, along the lines of "pinch the nose and blow into the mouth". Dad had to struggle to unlock my mouth in order to free the airway and in doing so cut his hand on the edge of my teeth before giving me mouth-to-mouth resuscitation to revive me. The man who helped Dad also rang the Knightsbridge Fire Brigade stationed a few doors away. They came with some breathing apparatus to give some assistance but it wasn't required. When I came round I got a lot of phlegm up, combined with the pinky colouration of the expectorant. Mum then phoned Professor Edwards and we managed to get through to him. We told him what had happened and which hospital we were going to. One of Prof's colleagues, a Dr. Carol, then chatted to a doctor at the Westminster Hospital. I had some treatment in the casualty department of the hospital, which included my stomach being pumped to remove some wind before spending a few days under observation.

Whilst I was in the Westminster I had a few tests, one of which was a video endoscopy which recorded me swallowing various textures of food to find out how the food went down the throat. The outcome of this was, from that time on, all my food had to be semi-liquidised. The medics also advised me to take a sip of water between each morsel of food in order to push the food down. During my stay at the hospital I had very little sleep and not much food.

We travelled home from the hospital on the Wednesday before Easter and had a good journey back. However, when it came to my first "meal" it was decided to have bits of bread marinated in 'le Bovril' and tinned plum tomatoes – not forgetting the sips of water in between each morsel. Things became quite difficult for a while with regard to the food being liquidised and this in turn caused a lot of discomfort for me with wind in my stomach, as this was a complete change in my eating habits. To relieve the wind I had to go on the loo a few times during the day. After eating, I got very breathless at times due to the accumulation of phlegm which was hard to clear and rather distressing. A physiotherapist taught Mum and Dad how to assist me in coughing and to help clear the phlegm. I also had some tablets to break down the secretions and help breathing. I found it effective. Our GP, Dr. Ramsdale came to see me at home and check things over a few days later. I began to use the ventilator for short periods of refreshment time which took quite a lot of time to get used to. I was also starting to use the machine for periods from 6.00am until I got up and dressed at 10.00am. It took some time for all of us to adjust and grow more confident with the routine. It is in times like these that my faith in God gave me the strength to cope and adapt.

The intercom from my room to upstairs coupled with the ripple bed noise was in competition with the purring of the ventilator; this was a matter of concern for Mum and Dad since they felt that my voice would not be heard from their bedroom. As a consequence of this it was decided that either Mum or Dad would sleep downstairs with me in my room. At this time I was using a ripple bed to sleep on and this was becoming quite uncomfortable, until the physiotherapist mentioned the use of a Roho mattress and seat which I found very comfy. A couple of weeks after having the Roho mattress I went through a period of feeling very tired and needing to sleep for more frequent periods. I would get into my chair for about five or ten minutes and feel breathless and need to lie down again with the ventilator. This happened about a month after my spell in hospital and continued for maybe two weeks. At this time, because my bowels weren't opening as well as they should even with suppositories, which I had been using since about 1983, I started taking two laxative tablets every three days or so, without which I would not be able to perform. Sometimes I took extra suppositories ('bullets') if my stools needed additional help.

Using the ventilator mask repeatedly over my nose, and at a

pressure sufficient to ensure a good air seal, caused an indentation over the bridge of my nose which eventually would break the surface of the skin and bleed. This was quite a problem since, as time went on, the interval off the ventilator was not long enough to allow healing to take place. This was despite the use of TCP (which "killed" when applied) and an adhesive tape with a towelling surface on the mask, the type used by tennis players on the handles of their racquets to absorb sweat from their hands. Tegaderm, another type of clear dressing tape recommended by our GP, proved very successful. At the time of writing, we use a combination of mostly Tegaderm and Duoderm dressing if things get very sore. A much improved softer mask design called a Gold Seal eventually became available in 1997. It continues to work very well, in conjunction with the dressing tapes.

As the summer of 1990 progressed the weather was very warm and humid; this affected my breathing again and in consequence more time was spent on the ventilator. As time went by things became more stable and I spent up to nine hours off the machine during the day but slept all night on it. Frequently this would lead to a build-up of wind due to swallowing air, so I would lie on my side off the machine for about 40 minutes in order to expel it. Sometimes, this procedure was not always successful, and the wind remained trapped until it was expelled by a session on the loo – a real relief experienced by all! When I am on the ventilator I take the opportunity of drinking as much liquid as I can, as it makes it easier with the extra air supply, giving me more breath. When off the ventilator I can only manage sips of liquid.

I went on a few day trips out during the summer of 1990 and decided to go for a weekend away to Glasgow in September as things became more stable. This took a lot of confidence. We took all our gear, Roho mattresses, ventilator, liquidiser etc. etc. We spent sometime in Glasgow visiting the Burrell Collection, with its many fine works of art, including the unusual sculptures in the garden by Henry Moore, a most interesting visit. We also spent some time along the western shores on the Bonnie Wee Banks of Loch Lomond. At 32 miles long the Loch is known as the Queen of the Scottish Lochs. It was most enjoyable to get away for a well-deserved break.

As this trip went so well we decided to go on a few more weekends away. We went to Bristol, visiting such sites as the Cheddar Gorge, Wells Cathedral, *SS Great Britain*, and the Avon Gorge including the Clifton Suspension Bridge, to mention just a few. On another weekend, we decided to go to Cardiff and the Gower Peninsula and another weekend we went to Southampton taking in the New Forest and Bournemouth. Very occasionally a problem would arise to affect my breathing. During the day I would have to be rushed through to my room because phlegm had accumulated more than usual, so it was necessary to go on my ventilator and bring loads of muck up until eventually it settled down. Then I would get back into my chair and continue with the day. On one occasion in 1992 when travelling to Exeter in the car, some phlegm built up which neither I nor Dad's racking would shift, so I asked Dad to stop at a nearby house, which was in the process of being painted on the outside, to ask whether the ventilator might be plugged in to their electricity supply. The people were most helpful in letting us lay out my Roho mattress on their living room floor. After a short time the muck cleared so then we continued on our journey to Devon.

In August 1993 I had a very nasty pressure sore on my bottom, which was very painful at times, often interrupting my sleep. Getting comfortable in bed was difficult, for it required that someone was awakened in order to make me comfortable. With the pressure sore it sometimes meant moving me up to 30 times during the night to ease the pain and restore my comfort. The cumulative effects of not sleeping very well over a period of months became very wearying. The district nurses had to come in daily to dress the area of the sore. This went on for several months and at one time the sore tunnelled down to the bone. For this our doctor prescribed a mild antibiotic which helped immensely. I also took the occasional pain killer. After about nine months the sore healed completely to the amazement of everyone. However, I now still have a dressing to protect the area.

Also in 1993 we had quite a number of power cuts at home because in our village the power cables are overhead and therefore vulnerable in extreme weather conditions. This prompted us to purchase a petrol-driven generator to provide a 240 volt supply. What a din this made, even though it was out in a shed with an extension lead to the ventilator in my room. One night, while Dad was away working, we had a power cut in the middle of the night, so Mum plugged everything in but could not start the generator up with the pull cord. After several unsuccessful attempts, she had an idea, why not ring the police on 999? They soon arrived, sorted the problem and waited to make sure everything was OK.

One night in November 1994 the ventilator broke down. Dad was away and we were unaware of a 24hr emergency contact number so we decided to phone 999 to get an ambulance. I was taken to the Countess of Chester Hospital sustained all the way with a supply of oxygen. Mum rang Professor Edwards from the hospital, who advised getting my ventilator from home to the hospital to see if they could do anything with it in the way of a repair. Mum collected it via a taxi, but it failed to run for more than a few minutes. I stayed up and upright all the night with no ventilator available to fit my needs. Amazingly I remained calm, my faith and trust in the Lord helped me through a difficult period. I gazed out of the window all night and watched the seagulls arriving in the morning. In the morning a technician called by, but in the absence of appropriate manuals could not fix it and decided to ring a physiotherapist for other ideas. The physiotherapist arrived with a Dr. Fergusson who made some observations of my breathing before trying a small portable device which delivered a continuous flow of air. I couldn't cope with this, since I needed the sequence of inhalation and exhalation. Dr. Fergusson said that if I became more breathless he would do something else. Eventually, the ventilator guy arrived from the service place, Deva Medical, who took away the faulty machine and left a replacement with us. Dad had driven up from Brixham in Devon and took us home for a well-earned rest and sleep!

Sometimes during the night I am awakened with the request, "Shut your mouth, Joni", meant in the best possible way for me to shut up! This happens when my mouth falls open, as happens with most of us when asleep, only in my case an open mouth causes the ventilator alarm to activate indicating a lowering of air pressure. This in turn, obviously interrupts my sleep pattern and anyone else who hears the alarm! Hence, "Shut your mouth!" It is a safety device for occasions such as power cuts, machine failure, or a simple leaking of air through a damaged pipe or seal.

In December 1994 a portable ventilator came on to the market so we immediately ordered one This ventilator has been absolutely great for me – it has made an enormous difference in my life, we can now travel far and wide on our breaks away in this country. It is most convenient for me as when we are travelling around I can go on the ventilator in the car and feel refreshed when I need to. I have a 60-hour power pack for the ventilator, but it will also work off the 12volt DC supply in a car. This machine and power pack makes life so much easier. The day after purchasing this equipment I had a bad cold and this ventilator was very beneficial in helping to clear phlegm coupled with good old honey and lemon! I also had to be racked (or postural drainage) to clear muck from my airways.

I had a physiotherapist in most days until the cold cleared. She also administered 'suction', not a pleasant experience having a tube inserted up the nose and into the throat.

In April 1996 I began to use this ventilator more during the day. I now use it on average 19 hours per day, although this varies slightly. In the Autumn of 1996 a new type of ventilator mask came on the market called "a jelly mask".

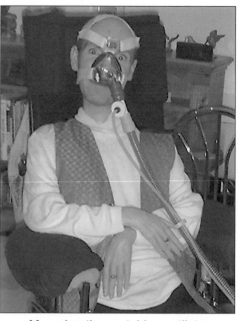
Me using the portable ventilator

It was a lot softer and therefore more comfortable to wear than previous designs, which tended to cut my nose more often.

Speaking of masks, that reminds me of a humorous encounter with a law enforcement officer, otherwise known as the police! Dad and I were coming back from a birdwatching trip to Beeston to see nesting Peregrine Falcons. We had just turned onto the A41 when a police patrol car with all its lights flashing appeared in the rear view mirror and indicated for us to pull over and stop. The policeman stepped out of the car with the full authority of a 'nick-nick' in prospect and asked, "everything all right?" He had spotted the mask on my head and wondered what was going on! Dad explained that the mask was part of the ventilator gear so after asking if I was OK (and hadn't been kidnapped) he bade us farewell. Life is not always what it seems, but he was a very observant policeman nevertheless.

Chapter 20

Diet and Routine

Whilst my activities in any week could be many and various, certain features of my routine are regular and 'fixed' - for example, washing. There is a 'loo' time of day, times to lie down and times to sit up, TV programmes to coincide with and so on. Below I have compared a typical day in 1991 followed by a typical day in 1996.

1991 – A day's routine (aged 24)

9.00am	Wake up, come round, and take a couple of drinks of fruit juice.
10.30-11am	Get out of bed and off the ventilator.
11.00am	Sit on commode for up to an hour to relieve wind.
12.00am	Get dressed.
12.20pm	Have breakfast of either Ready-Brek or a Marmite sandwich, occasionally, liquidised bacon with broken-up egg (after each morsel or two of food, I would drink a sip or mouthful of water to help the food go down).
12.45pm	Start of day's activities. i.e. reading, producing ink drawings, watching TV or videos.
2.00pm	Lunch e.g. Fisherman's Pie, followed by fruit yoghurt.
2.20pm	Resume activities.
5.30pm	Teatime. e.g. various sandwiches, soft cheese,

salmon paste, tarasamalata (a Greek fish dip) followed by chocolate mousse.

6.00pm   On the loo! To get rid of accumulated wind from the day.

6.20pm   Off the loo for a lie down and then back on ventilator for a refresh then have another drink.

7.10pm   Get up and watch TV or read.

10.00pm   Prepare for bed. Have a suppository followed by a spell on commode, then back into bed, get comfortable, and hooked up to ventilator and eventually to the land of Nod and Dreams.

Throughout the day had to be racked to clear muck as required, usually quite a number of times.

1996 – Typical day's routine (aged 29).

9.00am   Wake up, come round, have a chocolate or two After Eights and take a drink of fruit juice, then 20mins or so later have an Ensure liquid meal drink.

10.30-11am Get out of bed and off the main ventilator.

11.00am   Sit on commode and hook up to portable ventilator to clear muck. Once clear, stay off the ventilator for ¼ hour or so until need be. Duration on loo 1 hour

12.00am   Get dressed, shaved etc.

12.20pm   Blow nose to clear of as much muck as possible. This causes me to become "puffy" i.e. breathless. Hook up to ventilator.

12.25pm   Breath back! Have a few mouthfuls of water. Then into the day's activities. Reading and watching videos. At this point in time, I no longer had the strength to draw using the medium of ink.

12.50pm	Come off ventilator until feeling "puffy". Any length of time up to 15 minutes. Then back on ventilator.
1.05pm	Repeat this cycle throughout the day.
4.00pm	Go through to my room onto the commode to get wind out. At this point not on the ventilator. Stay on loo till breathing becomes difficult i.e. up to 50 minutes.
4.50pm	Into bed and onto main ventilator. Rest and Ensure liquid food drink. Get up after 45minutes on average.
5.35pm	Get out of bed and move into study onto portable ventilator, usually after five minutes, resume activities. Come on and off this ventilator until about 7.00pm.
7.00pm	Go through to my room and on to commode in order to clear wind.
7.20pm	Off the loo and into bed onto main ventilator. Rest and Ensure liquid food drink. Lie down for 45 minutes.
8.00pm	Get up, move into study, watch TV or read. On and off the ventilator throughout the evening.
10.00pm	Prepare for bed. Have a suppository followed by a spell on commode, then back into bed, get comfortable and hooked up to ventilator, and eventually go to sleep.

Towards the end of 1996 I found eating difficult and therefore not as enjoyable so I reverted to a liquid diet called Ensure. Originally we thought that the packs were meals in themselves and contained all the essential minerals, nutrients and elements to live on. However, this is not the case because they are only supplements so now (2002) I am drinking more supplements to rectify this and increasing my calorie intake. This also gives me a wider variety of different drinks.

It is essential to have a balanced diet – this is extremely important. In Muscular Dystrophy sufferers it is important also to keep a check on one's weight, so the diet should consist of a lot of protein. I had made use of Ensure in the past, it comes in several flavours, both savoury and sweet. I prefer the savoury flavours, asparagus, chicken and mushroom. To add to this I eat chocolate, soft cheese, such as Brie and Camembert, and Salmon Poacher which has a mousse-type texture. The texture is important, it minimises chewing and the risk of choking.

Chocolate is a preference for three reasons:
1. I like the taste!
2. I put on a bit of weight and
3. It helps to clear muck by binding it together.

Even so, there is no way I could swallow without drinking liquid fairly quickly, to help push the food down. I must stress that one needs to be very careful when eating food lying down because of the increased risk of choking.

As I write, I am drinking a lot more and a wide variety of liquids such as tomato juice, Bovril, and occasionally coffee, drinking chocolate together with other fruit juices which I have consumed for a long time now. Water, surprisingly, is harder to drink! The texture is less dense than other drinks and seems to slip down the throat too quickly. Sips are fine but larger volumes not so easy to handle. Most people will find drinking a pint of beer easier than a pint of water! I must emphasise the importance of drinking as much fluid as possible.

Chapter 21

Practical Tips, Advice and Personal Experiences

Coughs and colds

Colds and infections are always an issue: I have to be on my guard as infections can lead to extremely serious conditions. You can't be wrapped up in cotton wool, but you have to be careful.

On the occasions when I have had colds and infections my parents have to keep their distance as much as possible, when they are doing things for me they have to wear masks coated in Savlon making sure their mouths and noses are well covered to minimise infection.

As soon as I feel the first signs of a cold I go on antibiotics straight away to stave off further infection. I also struggle with the removal of phlegm.

For the past 17 years I have received the 'flu vaccination to minimise further infection. Sometimes I do take risks (not recklessly). The greatest risk in life is not taking risks.

Going out and about

I have to be careful in windy and cold conditions because it makes me breathless; to counteract this I stay on my ventilator, and if the winds are really strong my chair has to be turned so the back is against the wind. It is also not good to let the cold get to my chest When I do venture out in the cold I make sure I am well wrapped up with hat, gloves, scarf, etc.

Dental advice

Cleaning my teeth has become more difficult over the last 10 years, mainly due to breathing problems because it makes me breathless quickly, but it is an important job to perform, taking into consideration the fact that I suffer from gingivitis (inflammation of the gums). I have recently started to clean my teeth while on the ventilator but this proves difficult because the mask restricts how wide I can open my mouth. I also use a mouthwash after each cleaning to help prevent bacterial infection. This makes you feel refreshed and tingling!

Dressings

For ventilator users Tegaderm and Duoderm dressings are good to help make the mask more comfortable, coupled with nowadays, Mepore dressing on top of Tegaderm.

Socialising

It is important to socialise as much as possible. Always be in touch with your friends, and invite people to see you. Disabled people should be with non-handicapped people whenever possible, talking to them and mixing with them as much as they can.

Singing

1985 was a year when I started singing more which has been beneficial to my lungs and I felt a lot better for it. This was also something I enjoyed so much so that I chose to sing three songs as a party piece one Christmas Day evening at a family party the following year.

Sleep Studies

In September 1986 I was asked to take part in a sleep study by Professor Edward's Muscular Dystrophy research team at Fazakerley Hospital Liverpool, which would run for two nights. They were investigating blood oxygen levels during sleep coupled with sleep patterns. Getting ready for bed required more than pyjamas! I had to be wired up to electrodes with a tube surrounding the nose to monitor the dynamics of respiration and other wiring to the side of my head. They also attached a 24hr ECG (electrocardiograph) to record the heart during sleep. The results were recorded by a multi-pen-chart recorder and produced volumes of paper, quite a job for those who had to interpret the data. Rather them than me!

Incidentally, during sleep, we all dream during the REM (Rapid Eye Movement) period of sleep, when breathing levels drop.

I remember well the time that the pads on my chest came to be removed by a rather attractive physiotherapist. She apologised and asked me not to be rude to her as she ripped off the pads with a skilful flick of her fingers. It wasn't too painful, but I lost a few hairs from my hairy chest! Further tests followed including taking blood from my groin region before I was finally discharged.

The sleep study at Fazakerley was carried out on a chest ward and a few days later I contracted a chest infection which took three weeks to clear up.

In 1988/early '89 I was involved with a few more sleep studies, this time carried out at home with more modern and portable equipment and the pen recorder only spilled out just one small piece of paper with all the results on ready for the medics to interpret. The tests at home seemed more natural and provided valuable information for my future needs i.e. help with lung function (see chapter on Ventilation).

Sleeping

It is extremely important when lying in bed and on your back to keep your knees together. Some Muscular Dystrophy sufferers lie with their knees apart, which causes muscles to "fix" in this position and in time to make sitting more difficult and uncomfortable. When lying on your side and back it is important to lie as straight as possible.

For many years I slept on my right side and on my back on a conventional mattress because I find it uncomfortable on my left side. On my side I lie as straight as possible with my legs and knees on top of each other. It takes a bit of time to get comfortable however; when I lie on my back I lie with my legs and knees together with a pillow propped underneath my knees and one at each side of them in a comfortable position. But it does take a bit of time to get comfy.

In 1985 I started using a ripple bed which we put underneath the sheet. It was electrically controlled and went up and down about every two to three minutes. It prevented me from getting bottom ache and pressure sores. I only used this on my back. It made me sleep for longer periods of time, which was better for Mum and Dad and for me. The ripple bed was plastic and made me very sweaty, particularly in the summer. Then in 1990 when the ripple bed was getting even more uncomfortable, I got a Roho mattress.

The Lake District, March 1993

In February 1993 a brochure arrived through our door advertising the Langdale Hotel and Country Club. Mum suggested going away with me for a four-day break. The following month off we went! Dad drove us there, and got all our gear together including my commode, since Mum found it difficult to lift and hold me on a conventional loo. We left home around 11.30am to travel up the M6 motorway, stopping off at the Forton Services where we had a sandwich lunch, then proceeded on to the lakes. The scenery was wonderful and typical for March, a little greenery, some blossom coming out with daffodils everywhere. We observed a few newborn spring lambs.

We arrived at the Langdale Hotel just on two o'clock. It was an absolutely wonderful spot. We booked in and Mum and Dad unloaded all the gear. That done we went for a short car trip, with me doing the navigating up the Great Langdale Valley. We saw the Dungeon Ghyll waterfall. We left the Langdale Valley up a very steep winding track-like road to a spot overlooking Blea Tarn. Looking back from this vantage point awesome views were gained of the mountains flanking us. Then we returned to the hotel.

Our chalet-like accommodation had a small balcony at the rear which overlooked the beck. The stream was very fast flowing with a few cascades and quite a bit of spray, a lovely sight. The room was beautifully furnished with attractive décor and drapery. After settling in we walked around the hotel grounds which were in keeping with the environment – lots of pine trees, a large lake and evidence of water mill workings, with huge millstones strewn about the place. After tea, in the early evening, Dad left us to drive back home.

We were up early next morning and went for a leisurely walk around. It was a very pleasant time, taking in the beauty of the area – the trees, the blossom, the spring flowers and the birds, including a lovely pheasant and its gaudy attire. We walked alongside part of the beck which flowed by our room and surged with more power today, due to the previous night's rainfall. Later whilst I was looking out over the beck I spotted two red squirrels which was very exciting. The rest of the stay was spent reading, walking around the complex when the weather was suitable, and generally relaxing into this tranquil setting, watching the changing moods of the stream. By the time our stay was over the water was raging and more voluminous.

After a pleasant few days, from our arrival on Sunday through to Thursday, the time simply flew by before Dad returned in the afternoon to pick us up and take us home, via Grasmere, after a relaxing break.

175

Respite Care

In the Autumn of 1997 Mum and Dad decided to find out about respite care. It was to be provided by a National Health Trust under the Care in the Community scheme. We decided to have six hours a week. The first respite carer was a lady called Liz who stayed with us for five months. She was nice and we got on well. My second carer was Pauline: we also got on well and had many things to share about the Christian faith -Pauline as a Catholic and I as a member of the Church of England, which led to interesting conversations. Pauline also read to me which was good. Even in her retirement she remains a loyal friend, calling in and we often speak on the phone.

The main things that a nurse or carer has to do for me in the case of an emergency such as a power cut, are to take me off the machine and make a transfer to a portable ventilator and its battery pack. Another part of their job is to wipe phlegm out of my mouth and move my hands and feet if they get uncomfy or sore.

More Consideration

I think the Government and Councils should be pressurised in making things easier and doing more for the disabled e.g., by making buildings more accessible and by putting more ramps about towns and cities, building more lifts, and spacing clothes and other items out more in shops so that you can get passed them more easily without you catching the goods. In the past, I have caught clothes in the wheels of my wheelchair which is rather embarrassing and other people find this just as difficult. I think the Government should bring a new Act through Parliament called "The More Consideration Act for the Disabled." I am not saying the Government doesn't do any-thing for the disabled, because it does a lot to help, but I do think it could do a lot more.

London

In 1998 we decided to look for a flat in London and were fortunate to find one overlooking the Thames in the vicinity of Limehouse. At this time my sister, Christine, was sharing a flat in West London. So after we'd purchased this flat my sister moved in. We would come around, my family and I, to visit from time to time. We have underground parking beneath the flat which means I am sheltered from the elements. There is a lift up to the flat on the first floor and it is equipped for me with a collapsible commode which makes things easier. My bed is large so Mum or Dad have to stretch over me to put my ventilator mask on and give me drinks etc. The streets nearby are wheelchair friendly, with nice flat pavements. When we visit the flat I particularly enjoy watching the birds from the window: various seagulls, swans, mallards, coots and cormorants galore! In addition to this the river traffic provides another pleasant dimension to our visits with large cargo barges, yachts, sight-seeing craft, occasional ocean-going liners and even rowing crews floating past. Nearby is the massive Canary Wharf development with numerous shops, cafés, restaurants and the like. The flat is an ideal location to get to bird-watching reserves in the area, such as the Lee Valley about 45 minutes away to the northwest. It also easy to get to the bird reserves in Kent.

One exciting visit to the flat was for the Millennium celebrations, starting on December 31, 1999. We shared the evening with friends watching from the flat window and observed the laser beam which the Queen used to switch on London's Millennium Beacon situated on a barge anchored in the Thames at Tower Bridge. Later, at nine o'clock we saw the Queen pass by on a cruiser on her way to the festivities in the Millennium Dome. We watched the TV coverage with anticipation as Big Ben chimed in the year 2000. There was a fantastic, electric atmosphere emanating from the TV, coupled with that from the crowds lining the Thames walkway and from the pub below. Fireworks were exploding everywhere, phosphorescent rays of every colour lit up the Millennium London skyline. A fitting way to celebrate, not forgetting the champagne and singing to Cliff Richard's Millennium prayer song, "The Lord's Prayer."

Joyful News, but an anxious Time

In 1999 my sister Christine broke the news to us that she thought she was pregnant. Christine had been for the basic tests and they had been confirmed as positive. The news was initially a shock to us all, not least to Christine, since she is a carrier of the Duchenne Muscular Dystrophy Gene (DMD). This meant undergoing several tests, with anxious waits between each test, in order to determine, firstly, whether the baby was a boy (boys only are susceptible to the defective gene). One of the first tests confirmed it was a boy, now, it was necessary to ascertain whether the DMD gene was present. A final painful test was needed called Chorionic Villus followed by another agonising wait for the results. When the result was made known, the baby boy, to be eventually named Nicolas, was clear of DMD! We were absolutely delighted and tears of Joy came to my eyes after much prayer during this time.

The pregnancy progressed well and the next time I saw Christine was when she came over for Mum's 60th birthday celebrations, looking mature and glowingly pregnant! Three months later the baby was born on 12th December 1999. After a long and difficult labour Christine presented to her husband Tim and to the world baby Nicolas Karl Jonathan Zimmermann. His third name was named after me, his uncle Joni. Mum went over to Berlin to see the baby, but I was unable to fly due to my breathing requirements and the problems associated with cabin pressure. The following April Christine brought Nicolas to see me and it was a real Joy to see him face to face – a lovely boy. It meant a lot to me being alive to see him and to observe his development. Nicolas provided a whole new experience for me being an uncle.

New Horizons

In was at the end of November 1999 that a friend offered to scan this autobiography into a computer using, the then, latest OCR (Optical Character Recognition) computer technology which he did. We then transferred it onto a floppy disk and worked on it using my sister's lap-top computer linked to another monitor. I would then read the text on the monitor and dictate additions using the composition facilities that the computer offered. The following May I purchased a desk-top PC armed with the latest gizmos. The computer certainly opened up a new horizon for me, not merely on this autobiography but the world of the Internet. It is particularly invaluable for my interest in bird watching, finding information for reserves and links to direct 24-hour bird sightings around the country. It is also good using the e-mail facility to contact people and for them to contact me. The latest technology will give me the opportunity to use the computer with the flick of a micro-switch attached to my wheelchair and operated with the slightest movement of my left ankle, which therefore gives me more independence.

Possum Systems (for communication and independence)

I had heard about Possum systems a long time before we made contact with them. My basic requirements were for inter-communication, security and greater independence. Possum arranged for two advisors from a company called EAT (Electronic Assisted Technology) to come and assess my needs then they got back in touch with Possum who installed the hardware which comprised a compact control receiver unit operated from an infra red transmitter. In order for me to use the system a micro-switch on the end of a flexible cable was attached to my wheelchair which terminated close to my foot. It only required a light movement form my ankle to activate the system. This enabled me to use the telephone without anyone holding the receiver for me, which is great – it gives me more privacy to ring friends at home and abroad, such as my sister Christine, still currently living in Germany. Other useful features include a pager which enables me to bleep people when required, and to operate the CD player, TV, video and Sky Digital.

Possum provides us with technical back-up in the form of a man called Jim who installed the system in the beginning and continues to monitor its performance generally, fine-tuning it to my needs. He is a very obliging and helpful guy who speaks to me face to face. I found it difficult to operate "the switch" when lying down, since my foot would slip away from the micro-switch. So Jim came up with the idea of activating the system by frowning. Electrode pads were velcroed above my eyebrows. We discovered this was too sensitive and often triggered by involuntary facial movements, even slight vibrations from the inhalation and exhalation of air from the ventilator were sufficient to activate the system. Eventually, we tried a voice-operated means of control which works well, and we are able to adjust the sensitivity and the response time. I use this mainly when lying down, e.g. to bleep the pager, put on lights or control my stereo. Incidentally, Possum is the Latin word for "I can" or "I am able", so it's an apt name for the company.

Wheelchairs

Back in 1994 I decided that a new wheelchair was needed so I got in touch with a company specialising in wheelchairs. The one that eventually came was quite unsuitable for my needs and in the end the company was unable to supply me with a chair to suit my particular requirements. It was a physiotherapist friend from Hebden Green who recommended another firm who came up with the goods. A guy came out and took measurements from my existing electric chair to achieve the correct dimensions and added additional features such as head wedge supports, attached with Velcro to prevent my head falling from one side to another. In my experience wheelchair technicians – and this may sound like a generalisation – though well-meaning in trying to be helpful, don't understand the needs of a wheelchair occupant quite as well as the actual user, the exceptions being the guy mentioned above. After all the wheelchair needs to be as comfortable as possible for the user in a variety of ways, situations and uses. For example, for dining, reclining, reading, painting, outdoor use and a plethora of other activities.

TXI taxi

During the summer of 2002 I had a further experience using a local taxi firm; the taxi drivers were very helpful and supportive. The TXI taxi is specially adapted to take wheelchairs by using portable ramps. A feature on my wheelchair was a high headrest, so the TXI with its increased headroom was ideal to accommodate the wheelchair without too much trouble. This gave me greater independence and mobility since before the TXI it was only my Dad who was able to transport me in his car on trips out and weekends away. Now, Mum can take me out and about without lifting me from the chair and the risk of straining her back and mine!

My friend and companion, Paul

I first met Paul Haskew at the Christmas 1985 Barrow Church choir party held at The Manor House, the home of Tim and Eileen Healey. Mum sang in the choir with Paul but we didn't develop a close friendship until much later.

It was just after Christmas 1988 when I was partying at my good friend Edward's homestead, that I struck up a good conversation with Paul. We chatted for quite some time about Christianity mainly and found that we had many things in common – but not so many physical things, as I am much better looking than Paul!

The following Sunday I arranged for Paul to come around to my house and this initiated him coming on a regular basis to see me. We would chat on all manner of subjects, share our Faith in Jesus, read God's word together and pray through areas of concern. In addition we would read together a large number of books on Spiritual and Bible-related topics.

Paul has accompanied Dad and me on a few birdwatching outings as well weekends away in the Lake District and London. A good time has been had by all!

At the time of writing Paul has been a loyal friend for over 13 years. He has been a tremendous help with the computer and this autobiography.

A place to call my own

During the autumn of 2002 I moved into a ground floor flat (bachelor pad) near to Chester, with the support of Mum and Dad and my carer. It's a new experience having a place to call my own even though it is on rental. Buying new furniture and accessories for the flat has been great fun.

The flat has wooden floors throughout which is an ideal surface for manoeuvring my wheelchair. Inside is very spacious, and being open plan gives me plenty of room to accommodate all my personal possessions and ventilators, without the rooms being too big. The temperature also keeps at an even keel.

The flat is ideally situated within walking distance of Chester – it takes about a quarter of an hour to walk into the city centre. I go via the canal tow-path as it has flat even pathways which make it a pleasant walk. I also have the great expe-

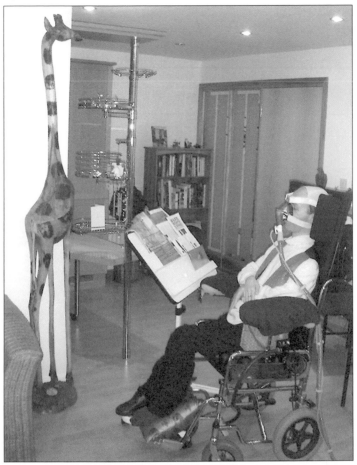

Me in my new 'bachelor pad'

rience of viewing the many barges that pass me by along their way. In addition to the barges I have spotted swans and other wild fowl splashing about with their young and I can observe more urban birds – YES!!!

I have my bird feeder and bird table outside the lounge window of my flat, which brings me great enjoyment.

Summary of key events

Age 5:	Diagnosis of Duchenne Muscular Dystrophy.

Age 5:   Used a bicycle with stabilizers.

Age 5:   Attained 10 metre swimming badge.

Age 9:   Used the wheelchair occasionally at school.

Age 10:   Wheelchair bound.

Age 15:   Back operation.

Age 16:   Painting on stones, slates and on paper.

Age 20:   No longer physically able to paint.

Age 22:   Ventilator used for the first time on average
9hrs   in 24hrs.

Age 23:   Resumed an earlier, less physically demanding,
             interest for pen and ink drawings.

Age 27:   No longer able, physically, to manipulate and
             coordinate the pen for ink drawing.

Age 27:   A portable ventilator came on the market and
             was purchased. It was a great liberator in that I
             could leave home for day trips or weekends
             away.

Age 29:   A full liquid diet of 'Ensure', supplemented
             with small amounts of cheese, chocolate, and
             mousse-like 'salmon poacher'.

Age 29:   Time off ventilator: maximum 5hrs in 24hrs*.

Age 34:   Review of my diet/calorie intake, resulting in a
             substantial increase of calorie intake and of
             course energy.

Age 35:   Time off ventilator: maximum just over 3½ hrs
             in 24hrs.

* Footnote: My time off the ventilator varies according to the atmospheric conditions such as temperature, humidity, wet weather and of course whether or not I have a cold.

184